The Swastika against the Cross
The Nazi War on Christianity

Bruce Walker

Outskirts Press, Inc.
Denver, Colorado

The Swastika against the Cross
The Nazi War on Christianity

Outskirts Press, Inc.
http://www.outskirtspress.com

ISBN: 978-1-4327-2169-5

Outskirts Press and the "OP" logo are trademarks belonging to Outskirts Press, Inc.

PRINTED IN THE UNITED STATES OF AMERICA

Preface

History has largely ignored the Nazi war on Christianity. Germany, before the Nazis came to power, is usually considered to have been a "Christian" nation, so many people assume that the German people before Hitler came to power were predominately Christian. The Nazi Party Platform also endorses something called "positive Christianity." It is easy to find photographs of Hitler at religious services. He often spoke about "God" and the "Almighty." Even a serious student of history might assume that there was a friendly connection between Nazism and Christianity. Nazis also tried to pretend that they did not persecute Christianity. Because so many people now reveal an almost visceral hatred of the Christian faith, any Nazi lie – even when the Nazis boasted about their willingness to lie – is accepted as Gospel by haters of Christianity.

Yet anyone with any knowledge of the tenets of Christianity knows how utterly incompatible Christianity is with Nazism. No major religion in human history is as completely at odds with Nazism as is Christianity. How, then, are these two opinions to be reconciled? How can a Christian nation have given rise to an odious movement so totally opposite from Christianity?

This book answers that question. There are a series of

points that progressively lead to the truth. Europe, to a large extent, had begun to abandon Christianity in the decades leading up to the rise of Nazism (and that trend has continued to the point that Europe today is largely de-Christianized.) Germany, in particular, had begun to abandon Christianity in the decades before Hitler came to power. The Nazis did embrace a sort of materialistic religion, but that religion was emphatically not Christianity. The religion of the Nazis was much closer to Islam or Hinduism than it was to Christianity. The Nazis hated Christianity and were fairly open about that fact. Part of the reason that the Nazis hated Jews so much was because Jews were supposed to have "tricked" Aryans into accepting Christianity. Hitler used every device at his disposal to gain and to hold power, and that included trying to hijack Christianity and to turn it into something that it never was and never could be.

The Nazis warred on traditional Christianity, and there is no doubt that Christianity itself would have faced a Nazi holocaust had the Nazis not been defeated in war. Christians also resisted the Nazis and these Christians paid a terrible price for that defiance. Writers seventy years ago saw that if the Nazis were not defeated, if the Nazis in fact won the world war, that the only force of decency that would survive Nazism would be Christianity. *Swastika Night* was written in 1937, a year before Kristallnacht, and in that dystopian classic Christians survived without ration cards, as untouchables and outcasts, but Christians alone remained immune to the evils of Nazism.

Fiction followed history, as this book reveals. The salient fact about the relationship between Nazism and Christianity is that Christianity proved the only force that Nazis would not cow into complete submission. But the Nazis tried very hard to end Christianity.

Introduction

This book has only a few points to make, and because those points are often contrary to what most people have come to believe, I use as references to back up my points old books. These books were generally written before the Second World War ended and in many cases the books were written before the Second World War had begun. As you read the book, remember that: The authors of these books had no idea how history would unfold; they did not know that the world would be plunged into global war or that six million Jews would be exterminated in horrific fashion. The authors of these books came from a variety of nationalities, religious beliefs and political views. Yet all of the authors agreed on the critical points in my book. I cite many authors to demonstrate the same point. I use evidentiary "overkill," because the purpose of this book is to leave the reader in absolutely no doubt about the relationship between Christianity and Nazism.

The book is not intended to present the whole interrelationship between Nazism and Christianity. Bad Christians collaborated with the Nazis and somehow reconciled that to their faith. But as the authors of these books again and again relate, Christianity and devout Christians were considered by the Nazis to be their enemy and the only people who stood up to the Nazis were Christians and those who genuinely believed in Christianity overwhelmingly resisted the Nazis. Nazism was not the result of too much Christianity; it was a result of too little Christianity.

Chapter 1
Germany before the Nazis

The idea that Europe was a Christian continent in the decades leading up to the Great War is more false than true. Europe itself had long been drifting toward open hostility to Christianity. This drift was closely tied to socialism and the rise of those sciences which led millions to believe that social engineering could replace the God of Christians and Jews. Lectures on socialism in the Nineteenth Century blamed poverty on Christianity. The same anti-Semitism of the late Nineteenth Century that led to scandals like the Dreyfus Affair in France was just as vicious toward Christianity. Hatred of Christianity and anti-Semitism went hand-in-hand.[1] The government of France before the Great War was just as hostile to Christianity as to Judaism.[2] The government of France had a cabinet office regulating religions called the Ministry of Cults. The leader of the so-called Right in France was a rabid opponent of Christianity and his articles about priests and nuns rivaled the pornographic and repulsive articles of Nazi Julius Streicher about lecherous Jews preying on innocent Aryan virgins.

---

[1] Michael Burleigh, *The Third Reich: A New History*, (New York: Hill and Wang, 2001), p. 96.

[2] John Mossie, *The Myth of the Great War* (New York: Harper-Collins, 2001), p. 26.

How early in modern history did Germany begin to reject Christianity? J. Salwyn Shapiro in his 1940 edition of *Modern and Contemporary European History* notes that Bismarck was bitterly anti-clerical and was little influenced by religion at all. Prussia, under Bismarck, in 1872 passed "May Laws" which required civil, rather than religious, marriages, which suppressed many religious orders, which resulted in the jailing of many clergymen, the confiscation of much church property and the closing of many churches.[3] Eugen Duhring, who wrote the very influential 1881 anti-Semitic tract, *The Jewish Question as a Racial, Moral and Cultural Problem* was a strong critic of Christianity.[4]

The cause of this decline was popular self-assurance that science or pseudo-science gave humanity, not some metaphysical Creator, the power to answer all the questions of man, provide for all the needs of man, and create Heaven on Earth. These were the decades during which Karl Marx and Charles Darwin captured the hearts and minds of men. Marx considered that Darwin's Theory of Evolution was the greatest scientific discovery of all time. God was unnecessary; man was self-made; the survival of the fittest was the preferred method of improving the human race provided by the only god that still existed – nature.

Hitler's ideas grew directly out of Marxism, although he rejected that incarnation of Marxism which was named Bolshevism (primarily because he considered it somehow Jewish.) Hitler also loved Darwinism. It was at the very heart of his odious racial theories. Those who rejected Darwinism and Marxism were serious Christians and Jews. Those who embraced Darwinism and Marxism were most

---

[3]   Salwyn Schapiro, *Modern and Contemporary European History*, (Cambridge, MA: The Riverside Press, 1940), pp. 392 – 393.

[4]   Jacob Marcus, *The Rise and Destiny of the German Jew*, (Cincinnati: Union of American Hebrew Congregation, 1934), p. 29.

typically those who hated Christianity and Judaism.

Germans accepted this more readily than almost any other people. "In 1906 the *Monistenbund* was founded in Germany with its anti-Christian tendencies and a campaign was launched against Christian education and its principles of charity and loving-kindness of alien races."[5] Price Collier in his 1913 book, *Germany and the Germans*, notes in the following passage how both anti-Semitism and anti-Christianity not only coexisted in Imperial Germany but that, indeed, the two noxious bigotries helped support each other: "The German sees a danger to his hardy own national life in the cosmopolitanism of the Jew; he sees a danger to his duty-doing, simple-living, and hard-working governing aristocracy in the tempting luxury of the recently rich Jew; and besides these objective reasons, he is instinctively antagonistic, as though he were born of the clouds of heaven and the Jew of clods of earth. This does not mean that the German is a believer, in the orthodox sense of the word, for this he is not. He loves the things of the mind not because he thinks of them as of divine creation, and as showing an allegiance to a divine Creator, but because they are the playthings of his own manufacture that amuse him most. His superiority to other nations is that he claims to enjoy maturer toys. Not even France is so entirely unencumbered by orthodox restraints in matters of faith...In Germany half-baked thinking, following upon, and as the result of, the barracks and corporal methods of education, have turned the Protestant population from the churches. The slovenly and patchy omniscience of the partly educated, leads them to believe that they know enough not to believe."[6]

---

[5]   Angelo S. Rappoport, *The Gauntlet Against the Gospel* (London: Skeffington & Son, p. 1937), p. 221.

[6]   Price Collier, *Germany and the Germans* (New York: Charles Scribner's Sons, 1913), pp. 166 – 167; p. 585.

That passage tells much. Germans and Frenchmen both stopped taking God seriously. Contempt for Jews is tied to that disbelief. Germans had begun to think that the world was their creation, and not the creation of God. The German toyed with life, which was filled with things to amuse him. Not only did this mean a rejection of the faith of the Jews, but it also meant a rejection of the faith of the Christians.

Germans had begun to view themselves as liberated from God. This nation which had produced a disproportionately large number of great thinkers and inventors came to view these very real achievements as shoving God out of their lives. One of the reasons why Christianity fell out of favor before the Great War was "To practice a religion which had been imported into Germany from abroad offended the pride of German intellectuals, philosophers, historians and scientists."[7] This was before the trauma of world war and the humiliation of the Treaty of Versailles.

During the First World War, Germans began in ever greater numbers to turn away from real religious faith, particularly Christianity. "Ludendorff regrets the fact that during the Great War Germany was still a Christian nation, although even then numerous Germans were Christian in name only."[8]

After the First World War, in the decades before the Nazis came to power, Christians more and more lost faith in Christianity. Germans began to formally leave the Christian faith in large numbers. In 1920 alone, more than 300,000 people formally resigned from the Christian faith.[9] During the years from 1918 to 1931, 2.4 million Evangelical Christians formally renounced their faith as well as al-

---

[7]   *The Gauntlet Against the Gospel*, Rappoport, p. 222.
[8]   *The Gauntlet Against the Gospel*, Rappoport, pp. 227.
[9]   Stewart Herman, *It's Your Souls We Want*, (New York: Harper & Brothers, 1943), 5.

most half a million Catholics. [10] As Paul Douglass notes in his 1935 book, *God among the Germans*, between 1908 and 1914, one hundred and fifteen thousand Christians in Germany formally renounced their faith; between 1914 and 1918 another fifteen thousand renounced their Christianity. After the First World War, Protestants were formally abandoning Christianity at an average annual rate of 186,000 per year, and Catholics at a somewhat lower level. [11] According to Douglass, between sixty-six percent and eighty percent of Germans who were nominally Christian when Hitler came to power had stopped taking communion. [12]

Martin Niemoeller, when the two were at Moabit Prison, told Leo Stein the condition of Christianity in Germany before the Nazis came to power "There was a serious decline in religion, and the decline was increasing. Communistic labor unions fought against the Church savagely. The masses were influenced by fiery speeches against religion, and notary publics were at hand who for a fee of two marks would receipt exemptions from church memberships. These receipts were valid under the law, and thus there was an almost daily decrease in church memberships. In Berlin alone, at a single meeting, many hundreds availed themselves of the easy opportunity to void their church memberships." [13]

In addition to this significant drop in the number of people in Germany who called themselves Christians, those remaining nominal Christians essentially stopped going to church. In Prussia, only 21% of the population took communion and in Hamburg only five percent of the population

---

[10] Richard Overy, *The Dictators*, (New York: W.W. Norton, 2004), pp. 278-279.

[11] Paul Douglass, *God among the Germans*, (Philadelphia: University of Pennsylvania Press, 1935), p. 278.

[12] *God among the Germans*, Douglass, pp. 278-279.

[13] Leo Stein, *I was in Hell with Niemoeller* (New York: Fleming Revell, 1942), p. 71.

took communion. "In Neu-Kolln, a worker's suburb of Berlin, less than one out of a hundred families attend Sunday services. About 10 per cent of the congregations was all that pastors could see in larger Hessian cities." [14] "While the recession in religious fervor was most evident in the large cities, particularly Berlin and Hamburg, it was noticeable throughout the country."[15] "(It is said that parishes in which perhaps one hundred will be the average Sunday attendance may have anywhere from 10,000 to 25,000 'members.')"[16] "Only a small proportion of the 40,000,000 Evangelicals went regularly to church."[17]

This movement away from Christianity was noted by authors writing about Germany at the time. Professor Henri Lichtenberger in his 1937 book, *The Third Reich*, describes the religious life of the Weimar Republic: "The large cities became 'spiritual cemeteries' in which there were hardly any believers apart from the official work with still professed a strict evangelical faith. The enlightened bourgeoisie, by force of tradition and convenience, continued to associate religion with the important acts of life but in general it lost all living faith. The working masses, influenced by socialism as well as of their own accord, were suspicious of the past as an accessory to the gendarme and of the church as working for the safety of the throne and security of the moneyed interest. Even in the country the sermons of the preacher did not seem to have much influence on the peasant or on public morality."[18]

---

[14]   George Schuster, *Like a Mighty Army* (New York: Appleton-Century, 1935), p. 97.

[15]   *Like a Mighty Army,* Schuster, p. 97.

[16]   Charles MacFarland, *The New Church and the New Germany,* (New York: MacMillan Company, 1934), p. 37.

[17]   Michael Power, *Religion in the Reich,* (Oxford, England: Kemp Hall Press, 1939), p. 100.

[18]   Henri Lichtenberger, *The Third Reich* (New York: The Greystone Press, 1937), pp. 188 – 189.

In 1938, Sidney Dark and R.S. Essex, discussing the spiritual condition of Germany before the Nazis, wrote: "The Evangelical Church seemed to have lost its vitality. At the beginning of the Nazi regime its services were lifeless, its teachings out of touch with modern thought, its pastors had little understanding of the needs of the young."[19] And the very same year, Mower wrote: "By 1920 God, and with him certainty, seemed to have withdrawn. The respectable subject suddenly awoke to the disintegration of standards that had been proceeding steadily since about 1860. First religion; the hold of Christianity over its followers had grown steadily weaker. One need only refer to the influence of such men as Comte, Darwin, Spencer and Hackel. Next, art had sickened, integral style giving way to eclecticism, atonal music, cubism, futurism, experimental literature."[20]

Weimar Germany was not a "Christian Nation" and the Weimar Germans were not a "Christian People." Millions of people, out of a population of about eighty million, were going to the trouble of formally renouncing their Christianity. Only a small percentage of those who remained nominal Christians bothered to go to church. Cities had become "spiritual cemeteries" and church services had become "lifeless." God Himself seemed to have withdrawn from Germany – thirteen years before the Nazis came to power.

This was reflected in the amoral behavior of the German people. Premarital sex by high school students was commonplace. Abortions were also commonplace. Pornographic entertainment was everywhere. Art had become sickening, music had become atonal, and those conventions we associate with faith had died. This was Germany before

---

[19] Sidney Dark and R.S. Essex, *The War Against God* (New York: Abington House, 1938) p. 149.

[20] Edgar Mower, *Germany Puts Back The Clock*, (New York: William Morrow Company, 1939), pp. 147 – 154.

the Nazis came to power. This was the condition of the German people who allowed Hitler to come to power. Germany had become indifferent or hostile to Christianity, just as it had long been indifferent or hostile to Judaism: the Judeo-Christian faith was held in contempt by the German people before Hitler rose to power.

Chapter 2
The Nazis and
Non Judeo-Christian Religion

Those who wish to tie Hitler to Christianity often note that he made references to the Almighty or to Providence in his speeches, invoking the name of God. This had nothing to do with Christianity and everything to do with his own religious beliefs, which were anything but Christian: "As self-appointed high priest of the German people, Adolph Hitler concluded many of his public addresses with an invocation to Providence. This intercession was usually offered in the form of a thinly-veiled ultimatum to the effect that the Nazi state, in its heroically titanic exertions to establish a New Order, expected the Almighty to do his Germanic duty. It is interesting to note that Hitler, in his last will and testament to the world before his death, left out this lip service."[21]

What was true of Hitler was true of Nazism in general: "Today the name 'Gott' in Germany is an empty world into which any concept can be poured. The polite references to God in the public speeches of Nazi leaders are, for the most part, a cynical concession to the credulity of the masses, not unlike the pious pretensions made by politicians every-

---

[21]   Stewart Herman, *The Rebirth of the German Church,* (New York: Harper Brothers, 1946), p. 78.

where in the world over, except perhaps in Russia where, it may be assumed, the name has been stricken from the vocabulary."[22]

Krzeniski noted much the same thing in his 1945 book, *National Cultures, Nazism and the Church*: "To be exact, Hitler does not limit himself to the use of the Divine in isolated instances. The term 'God' appears often in his speeches. Whether Hitler really thinks of God when he uses the term, or whether he employs it simply as a rhetorical ornament, is immaterial. The decisive test is the absolute denial of personal God implied in Racism. The God that Hitler invokes cannot be the true God, but must be a new God created by the Nazis."[23]

Wythe, in his book, *Riddle of the Reich*, expands on that idea: "If the outside world charges Nazism with being a religion, the Nazis are not at all upset. They second the motion most belligerently. In 1934, at Stuttgart, while administering the oath to the Conference of Nazi Bishops, this pronunciamento came from Bishop Jaeger: 'The German government must do away with the gospels completely and thus put an end to the religious divisions now plaguing the German people. The result will be a National Socialist Church.' Certain Nazis would not use Christianity as even a point of departure. To them the least borrowing from the Christian churches is anathema."[24]

What was this Nazi religion? As I will show in the next chapter, the religion of the Nazis bore no resemblance to the faith of true Christians or Jews. The Nazi faith, however, did bear a resemblance to religions outside Judeo-Christianity. Hitler said in 1943 that Nazis could be Mos-

---

[22] *It's Your Souls We Want*, Herman, pp. 62-63.
[23] Andrew Krzeninski, *National Cultures, Nazism and the Church* (Boston: Bruce Humphries, 1945), p. 46.
[24] William Wythe and Albert Parry, *Riddle of the Reich*, (New York: Prentice Hall, 1941), p. 144.

lems and be could Nazis.[25]

In 1938, R.H. Lockhart stated in his book, *Guns or Butter?* that Frenchmen were writing home from Nazi Germany "Everything is moving toward a supreme conflict between the Christian world and the new Islam." He went on to note that British and American businessmen, diplomats and journalists also began to view Nazism as a new Islam.[26] Lockhard also viewed books published by the Nazis that included *All-Islam: World Power of Tomorrow.*[27]

Himmler hated Christianity but he liked Islam. He met and liked the Grand Mufti. Hitler met that Moslem leader as well. Obergruppenfuhrer Gottlob Berger boasted: "A link is created between Islam and National-Socialism on an open, honest basis. It will be directed in terms of blood and race from the North, and in the ideological-spiritual sphere from the East."

When Hitler came to power, Jajj Amin el-Husseini as Mufti of Jerusalem called for jihad to eliminate all the Jews in Palestine. Moslems were recruited and volunteered to serve in the SS Handzar Division. Moslems even helped run the ghastly Jasenovac concentration camp, where over 10,000 Jews and over 40,000 Christians were murdered by the Nazis and their Islamic allies. Persian Shiite Moslems speculated that Hitler might be the Twelfth Prophet of Islam.[28]

Nazism and Islam fit together very well. Both hated Christians and Jews. Both believed that God wanted adherents to impose their will by violence upon the rest of the world and that this warring on the rest of humanity was di-

---

[25] Byran Mark Rigg, *Hitler's Jewish Soldiers* (Lawrence, KS: University of Kansas Press, 2002), pp. 18 – 19.

[26] R.H. Lockhardt, *Guns or Butter?* (London: Putnam, 1938) pp. 412 – 413; see also footnote 1, p. 413.

[27] *Guns or Butter?* Lockhardt, p. 411.

[28] John Lukács, *The Last European War* (New Haven, CT: Yale University Press, 1976), p. 476, footnote 64.

vinely inspired. Both rejected what we would call "Western Civilization."

Nazis also liked Eastern religions. Nazis sent missions to Tibet to find their "Aryan" roots in that Buddhist land. Savriti Devi, sometimes called "Hitler's Priestess" was a militant Hindu, who wrote books like *Warning to Hindus*. In that book Devi warns Indians against the dangers posed by Christian missionaries performing acts of compassion in India.

Himmler could quote extensively from the *Bhagavad Gita* and he was very familiar with both Buddhism and Hinduism. He guided the Nazis to seek their racial roots in Buddhist Tibet, where Nazis were generally well received. SS officers regularly meditated according to the Hindu and Buddhist practices at Schutzstaffel offices. In death camps, Schutzstaffel officers were told that killing Jews, "untouchables," actually helped these Jews by allowing them to be reincarnated into a higher caste.

Wilhelm Hauer, one of the leading Nazi metaphysical instructors and leader of the German Faith Movement (a pagan and overtly anti-Christian movement), was deeply reverent toward and knowledgeable about Buddhism.[29] This movement explains: "It follows that the Near-Eastern-Semitic and the Indo-German beliefs must stand against each other in a mighty struggle. This struggle is the theme of religious world history for the last thousands of years, and may perhaps remain so in the future. The struggle between Christianity and the German Faith in the German soul is thus an event of unsuspected depth."[30]

Nazis looked for an Indo-German belief system, a system which led Nazis into long, deep and expensive trips to

---

[29] Stephan Roberts, *The House That Hitler Built*, (London: Methuen, 1939), p. 276.

[30] Dark, Sidney and Essex, R.S., *The War Against God* (New York: Abington House, 1938), p. 165.

Tibet and exploration and collaboration with Indian nationalists and respect for Hinduism and Buddhism, in contrast to "Near-Eastern-Semitic belief" (Christianity and Judaism). This was reciprocated. The overwhelming majority of Dalits or "untouchables" in India are attracted to Christianity and against Hinduism (or Brahmanism) specifically because the Hindu belief in the spiritual caste into which one is born may not be altered in this lifetime. This attitude of hundreds of millions of Hindus today is almost identical to how Nazis viewed Jews or Slavs. It is not coincidence that Hitler was worshipped in many Indian homes as one of the gods of Hinduism.

Chapter 3
The Nazis and Christianity

If there is anything clear about the Nazis, it was that they hated the Jews and certainly this extended to a hatred of Judaism, the historical faith of the Jewish people. But the Nazis also hated Christianity. Nazis, more than most Germans, were hostile or indifferent to Christianity. Hitler originally appeared to just ignore Christianity. Dark and Essex write in their 1938 book that *Mein Kampf* has few passages which in any way refer to religion, none that refer to Hitler's own personal religion, or to the teaching of the Bible, nor any branch of Christian teaching.[31]

But within a year of taking power, Hitler was saying: "Christianity was incapable of uniting the Germans, and that only an entirely new world-theory was capable of doing so." This was not only the position of Hitler, but also the Nazi-supports "German Faith Movement," whose leader, Dr. Kraus, on November 13, 1933 said: "Hereafter there would be no admixture of 'foreign elements' in the 'German religion.' The Old Testament must be repudiated; the New must be 'cleansed of disfiguring passages,' and there must be in the Church no persons of alien blood. The

---

[31]   *The War Against God*, Dark and Essex, pp. 147 - 171.

speaker closed by shouting 'We reject the crucifix!'"[32]

Hitler told Martin Niemoeller in 1934: "Jesus Christ was only a man, and a Jew to boot. Why shouldn't I, who am more powerful than Christ, and who am able to be much more helpful than he – why shouldn't I have the right to establish a new dogma for the Church?"[33] Hitler went on to say: "My aim is to make Germany the only power in the world. I must, therefore, eliminate any kind of sickness, and I consider the sentimental feeling for Christianity as a kind of mental sickness."[34] Christianity was a sickness to Hitler, and he had definite ideas about how to deal with sickness and infirmity.

The other Nazi leaders were even more hostile to Christianity than Hitler. Martin Bormann especially hated Christianity. Goebbels frequently made fun of Christian morality. Nazis in general considered Christianity a "soul malady," "foreign" and "unnatural." Heinrich Himmler despised Christianity and members of the SS had to formally renounce their Christian faith and formally become agnostic in order to become a member of the Schutzstaffel.[35] Himmler wrote: "How different is yon Pale Figure on the Cross, whose passivity and emphasized suffering expressed only humility and self-abnegation, qualities which our heroic blood utterly deny...The corruption of our blood by the intrusion of this alien philosophy must be ended."[36]

Even Nazi leaders like Goring, who tried to stay out of the religion issue, on July 15, 1935 wrote in a circular: "It has come to the point where Catholic believers carry away

---

[32]   *Like a Mighty Army,* Schuster, p. 113.

[33]   Leo Stein, *I was in Hell with Niemoeller,* (New York: Fleming Revell, 18942), p. 90.

[34]   *I was in Hell with Niemoeller,* Stein, p. 91.

[35]   Alexander Rossino, *Hitler Strikes Poland* (Lawrence, KS: University of Kansas Press, 2003), pp. 32 - 40

[36]   Raymond Freely, *Nazism versus Religion,* (New York: The Paulist Press, 1940), p. 7.

but one impression from attendance at divine services and that is that the Catholic Church rejects the institutions of the National Socialist state. How could it be otherwise when they are continuously engaging in polemics on political questions or events in their sermons!"[37] Goring ordered that the *Hitler Gruss* (the Hitler salute) was the only religious gesture allowed. Duncan-Jones wrote of the Nazi Labour Front leader: "Dr. Ley, the energetic leader of the Labour Front, is one of the most powerful personalities in the Party Directorate, and one of the most contemptuous opponents of the Churches."[38] Nazi leader Binve said "Hitler is a new, greater, a moral powerful Jesus Christ. Our God, our Pope, is Adolph Hitler."[39]

The *Judenfibel*, a schoolbook filled with hatred toward Jews which was used to teach in Nazified German schools, not only attacks Jews, but states: "The teaching of mercy and love for one's neighbor is foreign to the German race and the Sermon on the Mount is, according to Nordic sentiment, an ethic for cowards and idiots."[40] Hatred of Jews and hatred of Christians went hand in hand with the Nazis: Both practiced a religion which was contrary to everything that Nazism represented. The Nazis did not nuance their attack on Christianity – calling the Sermon on the Mount an ethic for cowards and idiots. *Nordland*, a Nazi magazine, called the Sermon on the Mount "the first Bolshevist manifesto."[41] The Nazis publics official anti-Christian materials like *Why No More Christianity*, by Hans Weidler, which

---

[37] Henri Lichtenberger, *The Third Reich*, (New York: The Greystone Press, 1937), p.210.

[38] A.S. Duncan-Jones, *The Struggle for Religious Freedom in Germany*, (London: Victor Gollancz, 1938), p. 178.

[39] *The History of Bigotry in America*, Myers, p. 389.

[40] Stewart Herman, *It's Your Souls We Want*, (New York: Harper and Brothers, 1943), p. 57.

[41] Dorothy Thompson, *Let the Record Speak*, (Boston: Houghton-Mifflin, 1939), p. 287.

asked: "Can there be anything lofty about a religion whose God came into the world only for suffering and who died on the cross the ignominious death of a criminal?"[42] On January 12, 1936, *Der Blitz* had the following: "The German people is no longer blinded by the illusions as at the time of the Reformation. It has come to recognize not only Judaism, but Christianity too, as foreign to its genius."[43]

If Hitler pretended not to oppose Christianity before the Nazis came to power, that was simply masking his true intentions, as he said in 1932: "The political victory can only follow if the fight is concentrated against the fewest possible enemies – for the time being, the Marxists and the Jews. Then will come the Reaktion, and the end of that will mean the end of the Christian Church...Whether it's the Old Testament or the New, or simply the sayings of Jesus...it's all the same Jewish swindle...We are not out against the hundred and one different kinds of Christianity, but against Christianity itself."[44]

The Twenty-Five Theses of the German Religion, a conscious modeling of the twenty-five points of the Nazi program stated: "The Ethic of the German Religion condemns all belief in inherited sin, as well as the Jewish-Christian teaching of a fallen world. Such a teaching is not only non-Germanic and non-German, it is immoral and nonreligious. Whoever preaches these menaces the morality of the people."[45] Krause was directly connected to Hitler, who wished to develop the so-called German Christians into an Aryan religion with the only the name "Christian" remaining of Christian faith. The statements of Krause speak for themselves. He demands"Christianity" without an Old Testament, with a cleansed New Testament and no crucifix. This

---

[42]   *Nazism versus Religion,* Freely, p. 21.
[43]   Carl Carmer, *The War Against God* (New York: Henry Holt, 1943), p. 6.
[44]   *The War Against God,* Carmer, pp. 2-5.
[45]   *The War Against God,* Dark and Essex, pp. 147 – 171.

was not Christianity at all, and the Nazis knew it.

Ludendorff, one of the earliest Nazi supporters from the days of the Beer Hall Putsch, wrote in the forward to his wife's book, *Salvation from Jesus*: "Christianity, as my wife has most convincing demonstrated, has destroyed the will of the German people, nay, of all peoples wherever it has penetrated."[46] His wife, in that book, went even further: "Christ did not live according to his teachings. He was a false prophet: he became involved with drinking. In fear he went from Jerusalem to Bethany. He was not dead. He uproots man from race, people, and custom. He was a jew and thus the source of every evil."[47] Ludendorff and his wife were not always welcome in the Nazi camp, but Ludendorff was the most important early supporter of the Nazis.

The German Nordic Religion, which was also embraced by the Nazi, also repudiated Christianity: "Dr. Felix Fischer-Dodeleben, author of The Outline of a German Nordic Religion, entirely repudiates the divinity of Jesus. He attacks the Old Testament in its entirety, and the greater part of the New Testament. The virtues taught by the Cross are a stumbling-block to Nazi youth."[48]

Jakob Wilhelm Hauer, head of the pro-Nazi German Faith Movement, said: "If the conviction that there is only one road to truth and one way to God constitutes an inalienable characteristic of Christianity, then Christianity is basically opposed to German genius. We are faced with a choice between an alien and a German faith. The German nature itself will decide the issue."[49]

How did Nazis feel about the German Faith Movement? It was: "Amply subsidized by the Reich government, its activities encompassed every field of human endeavor. No

---

[46]   *The War Against God*, Dark, pp. 176-177.
[47]   *The War Against God*, Dark, p. 177.
[48]   *The War Against God*, Dark, p. 173.
[49]   *It's Your Souls We Want*, Herman, p. 63.

amount of public money was spared to promote its growth, or to hire speakers and propagandists who delivered countless talks and lectures. Special meeting and academies were constantly convoked, while the printing presses were kept busy turning out books and pamphlets."[50]

In February 1937, Dr. Kerrl made a speech in which he said: "Bishop von Galen and Dr. Zoellner wanted to bring home to me what Christianity really is, namely, that it is a question of the acknowledgment of Jesus as the Son of God. This is ridiculous, quite unessential. The Apostle's Creed is no longer the statement of Christianity. There has now arisen a new authority concerning what Christ and Christianity really is. The new authority is Adolph Hitler."[51] In the same speech, Kerrl, who was Minister of Religion in the Third Reich, said that he openly rejected the Apostle's Creed, which had been a lynchpin of Christianity for almost two thousand years. He said that the question of Jesus being the Son of God was ridiculous. And he placed Hitler as the spiritual authority over religion in Germany.

Nazi professor Ernst Bergmann at the University of Leipzig described Christianity thus: "Christianity is especially alien to the German nature because it is the creation of a pre-eminently oriental mind and rests upon the sacred writing of the Jews. It contradicts, almost at every point, the German sense of custom and morality."[52] University Nazis in Keil wrote in 1935: "We Germans are heathens and want no more Jewish religion in our Germany. We no longer believe in the Holy Ghost; we believe in the Holy Blood."

This was felt within the Nazi terrorist organizations as well. The leader of a Black Shirt Battalion asked: "Who is the greater – Christ or Hitler? At his death Christ had

---

[50] *National Cultures, Nazism and the Church,* Krzeninski, p. 66.
[51] *Religion in the Reich,* Power, p. 141.
[52] *National Cultures, Nazism and the Church,* Krzeninski,, p. 54.

twelve apostles, but even they did not remain faithful. Hitler today has seventy million behind him. We cannot tolerate that another organization which is of a different spirit should go side by side with us. We must destroy it."[53] In the training camps of the Nazi Party it was repeatedly stated that National Socialism has three enemies: Judaism, Masonry and Christianity.[54]

MacFarland in his 1934 book also noted the problem that all Nazis had with Christianity when he describes a particular, small event. During the first year in which the Nazis came to power, MacFarland writes: "In one instance a National Socialist himself says that, without his knowledge, he was nominated to the parish church council and was willing to serve his party in that way until he discovered that he must take a Biblical oath, which he would not do because he was not a professing Christian.[55]

Some Nazis said that Christianity was irrelevant. Others went further. Alfred Rosenberg, Nazi theoretician, said that there was no place in the Third Reich for Christianity in any form. His ponderous tome, *The Myth of the Twentieth Century*, not only called for banning crucifixes from churches but also from village streets, and also for banning medieval images of Christ as the Lamb of God.[56]

Nazis published books with names like *Jesus Never Lived* and pamphlets that said "If Jehovah has lost all meaning for us Germans, the same must be said of Jesus Christ, his son. He does not possess those moral qualities which the Church claims for him. He certainly lacks those characteristics which he would require to be a true German. Indeed, he is as disappointing, if we read his record careful, as is his father."[57]

---

[53] *The War Against God*, Dark, p. 186.
[54] *Let the Record Speak*, Thompson, p. 289.
[55] *The New Church and the New Germany*, MacFarland, p. 38.
[56] E.O. Lorimer, *What Hitler Wants* (London: Penguin, 1939), p. 109.
[57] *Riddle of the Reich*, Williams and Parry, p. 142.

Nazi philosopher Bruno Armann in 1939 wrote: "In the future, there should be no university which would not have at least one chair in the Jewish question, which would make accessible the Jew-problem to each student, but simultaneously, from the point of view of Weltanschauung, would also be directed against Protestant and Catholic denominationalism."[58] The Nazis viewed Christianity the same way that they viewed Judaism.

Christ, to Nazis, was a nebbish. Hitler *was* their Christ. "A Nazi magazine commented on the Golden Rule in 1939: 'This fundamental law of Christianity completely contradicts our moral conscience, contradicts above all our warrior-like nature peculiar to the soul of our race.' Children were taught to pray to Hitler instead of to God. Grace before meals given to poor children by the Nazi Welfare Committee ended: 'For this food, my Fuehrer, my thanks I render.' Another official child's prayer ended: 'My Fuehrer, by Fuehrer, my faith and my light, Heil my Fuehrer.'"[59]

Nazi "services" replaced Christian services in those ceremonies of private life. Herman relates: "A tangible illustration of what was happening on the spiritual front is provided by the funeral problem. An increasing number of fatalities, particularly among the higher officers and the SS Elite, made it necessary to reach some decision about a suitable burial ceremony. Church services were out of the question and yet the new heroes could not be interned without a formula of farewell."[60]

And this Nazification of services not only included the end of life, but the beginning of life: "Secular baptismal ceremonies were heard of almost as soon as it became fashionable to be a Nazi, that is, in 1933. Babies were baptized

[58]   Max Weinreich, *Hitler's Professors*, (Yiddish Scientific Institute: New York, 1946), p. 83.

[59]   Ernst Raab, *The Anatomy of Nazism*, (New York: B'nai B'rith, 1962), pp. 17 - 26.

[60]   *It's Your Souls We Want*, Herman, p. 10.

as new hereditary links into the 'ancestral chain' and were charged to guard their blood 'so that descendants for a thousand years after you will be thankful to you – for God is pure blood!' I know that children of the fervid devotees of the cult of the swastika have been baptized according to this formula. Christening by water and the Holy Spirit is, of course, totally rejected."[61]

Naturally it also included marriage. Goebbels said: "The new Marriage Law of Greater Germany recognizes only one kind of marriage, namely, the wedding performed by a civil official in the name of the Reich."[62] Wythe noted in 1941: "Births, marriages, deaths and other solemnities are already marked in ancient ways, without benefit of Christian clergy."

The Nazi hatred of Christianity was recognized by almost everyone who studied Nazi Germany after the Nazis came to power. These chroniclers of the Nazi attitude toward Christianity were not all Christians. Although all the chroniclers, Christian or Jewish, reached the same conclusions.

Jacob Marcus in his 1934 book by the Union of American Hebrew Congregations notes that "Though his parents were both Catholics, Hitler himself has apparently no interest in any organized religion."[63] It is important to remember the time and context of this opinion: During the first year in which Hitler was in power, a leading Jewish scholar who had studied Hitler concluded that the Nazi leading had no interest in organized religion. Marcus also has an entire section in his book about Nazi "anti-Christian anti-Semitism" which points out (as many other authors did) that hatred of Jews and of Christians were inseparably

---

[61] *It's Your Souls We Want*, Herman, p. 22.

[62] *It's Your Souls We Want*, Herman, p. 37.

[63] *The Rise and Destiny of the German Jew*, Marcus, p. 38.

linked.[64] Jacob Marcus was a professor of Jewish history who wrote extensively as a Reform rabbi about the history of the Jews.

John Cournos, another Jewish author, in his 1938 book, *An Open Letter to Jews and Christians*, noted: "Hitler's rejection of Christ can therefore be easily understood."[65] Cournos goes on in speaking of Hitler and *Mein Kampf* to say: "It is no accident that the author of those lines shows no partiality either to the Jew or to the Christian who still espouses Christ, and persecutes them both equally."[66] Cournos does what many other writers at this point in history did: He connected Hitler's hatred of Jews and Judaism with his hatred of Christians and Christianity. Hitler was the anti-thesis of Judeo-Christianity. Cournos, in fact, uses the very term "Judeo-Christianity," or as he spells it "Judaeo-Christianity," to describe the enemy of Nazism and Communism.[67]

Max Weinreich, another Jewish scholar, wrote right after the war ended: "Drowning the Jews would bring the Reich a good deal closer to drowning Christianity, too, which would leave national socialism (sic) the complete conqueror of German souls"[68] and "It would lead us too far afield to elaborate on all phases of the Nazi fight against the Christian religion as an outgrowth of Judaism, a fight which was countenanced by Rosenberg even before the seizure of power."[69] Max Weinreich was a linguist who founded the YIVO Institute for Jewish Research in the

---

[64] *The Rise and Destiny of the German Jew*, Marcus, p. 45.
[65] John Cournos, *An Open Letter to Jews and Christians*, (New York: Oxford University Press, 1938), p. 11.
[66] *An Open Letter to Jews and Christians*, Cournos, p. 60.
[67] *An Open Letter to Jews and Christians*, Cournos, p. 29.
[68] Max Weinrich, *Hitler's Professors: The Part of Scholarship in Germany's Crimes Against the Jewish People*, (New York: Yiddish Scientific Institute, 1946), p. 20.
[69] *Hitler's Professors*, Weinberg, p. 62.

1920s and was its director for many years.

Gustavus Myers in this 1943 book, *The History of Bigotry in the United States*, wrote: "Early in the Nazi movement Hitler had avowed his scorn for Christianity. Teaching, as it did, precepts of mercy, he scoffed at it as effeminate and altogether incompatible with his war plans which called for, in his scheme, a virile German people insusceptible to ethics and compassion."[70] Myers notes the same thing in his book: "A host of books issued in Germany ridiculed Christian concepts. To the question it asked, 'Did Jesus ever live?' one book replied 'We say no." This book derided the New Testament ethics as fit only for 'morons and idiots.' Another book declared Christianity 'a Utopia born of the true Jewish spirit, to destroy people and turn them into will-less slaves.' Pronouncing Christianity 'debasing' a third book disavowed the God of the Bible as 'never congenial to the German.'"[71] Myers was an historian, a well known journalist and a member of the Socialist Party in America.

Micklem explains in his 1939 pamphlet, *National Socialism and Christianity:* "If the 'German Christians' represent the left wing of Protestantism, the right wing are those who stand in unswerving loyalty to the old confessions of the Church"[72] and he goes on to write: "All political questions are at bottom theological. The clash between National Socialism and the Christian church rests upon the incompatibility of two views of the world, two 'anthropologies.' In National Socialism there are no ultimate, universal standards. Right is defined as that which accords with the demands of the people's souls…The Church in Germany is of no mere ephemeral interest. It raises in an acute form an is-

---

[70]   Gustavus Myers, *The History of Bigotry in the United States*, (New York: Random House, 1943), p. 388.

[71]   *The History of Bigotry in America*, Myers, p. 389.

[72]   N. Micklem, *National Socialism and Christianity*, (Oxford: Oxford University Press, 1939), p. 23.

sue which both National Socialism and Bolshevism present to every country. What is to be the foundation of European civilization?"[73] Micklem was a college head at Oxford.

A.S. Duncan-Jones, the Dean of Chichester, in his 1938 book, *The Struggle for Religious Freedom in Germany*, notes that before taking power Hitler said: "I insist on the certainty that sooner or later, once we hold power, Christianity will be overcome. Of course, I myself am a heathen to the bone."[74] Duncan-Jones also writes of the Nazi position on Christianity "The complete opposition to Christianity is plain."[75]

Raymond Freely, a professor at the University of San Francisco and a Catholic priest wrote in his 1940 book, *Nazism versus Religion*, that: "Nazism will seek to exterminate Christianity if Nazism dominates Europe"[76] and later that: "Nazism is waging a death struggle against both the Catholic and the Evangelical or Protestant Church."[77]

Michael Power, in his 1939 book, *Religion in the Reich*, wrote: "There has probably been no more curious persecution in History than the attack made by National-Socialism upon the Christian Churches." Power was an eye witness to this persecution as he had just been through Germany before the Second World War started.

Paul Douglass, in his 1935 book, *God among the Germans*, writes that: "The first great struggle of ideologies within the folkic state of Adolph Hitler has come between a section of the Church of Jesus Christ and the National So-

[73] *National Socialism and Christianity*, Micklem, (Oxford: Oxford, 1939), p. 31.
[74] *The Struggle for Religious Freedom in Germany*, Duncan-Jones, p. 147.
[75] *The Struggle for Religious Freedom in Germany*, Duncan-Jones, p. 22.
[76] *Nazism versus Religion*, Freely, p. 3.
[77] *Nazism versus Religion*, Freely, p. 4.

cialist Government."[78] Douglass was a distinguished scholar whose book was published by the University of Pennsylvania.

The 1943 book, *Christian Counter-Attack*, puts it thus: "Beyond all question the Nazis are waging war upon the Christian faith and Christian values."[79] "When Hitler became Chancellor in January 1933, the main outlines of the Protestant front could already be discerned. On the extreme left was a body of so-called 'German Christians.' These were Church people who were fanatical Nazis, so fanatical indeed that they pictured a complete synthesis between Christianity and Nazism. They used a number of Christian expressions (for example, God and Christ), but their version of Christianity bore little resemblance to any of its known historic forms."[80] The four co-authors of this book were published by the Student Christian Movement Press.

Essex and Dark, in their 1938 book, *The War Against God*, wrote: "In Germany Christianity has been put on trial because it is a unifying force between nations, proclaiming, as it does, the equality of black and white, Jew and Gentile."[81] Sidney Dark was a British newspaper editor who wrote on a variety of topics for many years.

Rauschning in 1938 noted the same absolute hatred that the Nazis had for Christianity. He wrote: "The purpose of the National Socialism fight against Christianity is the same: the total destruction of the last and most deep-rooted support of the forces of conservation. The destruction of the spirit of Christianity in Germany is certainly more far-reaching than appears on the surface...Such vestiges of living Christianity as remain are steadily degenerating in the

---

[78] *God among the Germans*, Douglass, p. 10.
[79] Hugh Martin, Douglas Newton, H.M. Waddams and R.R. Williams, *Christian Counter-Attack: Europe's Churches Against Nazism*, (London: Student Christian Movement Press, 1943), p. 12.
[80] *Christian Counter-Attack*, Martin et al., p. 31.
[81] *The War Against God*, Essex and Dark, p. 145.

direction of a superficial and unthinking deism"[82] and that ultimate goal as "...the total abolition of Christianity, which is not a mere philosophical fad of the National Socialists but an iron necessity of their system."[83] Herman Rauschning had been a Nazi leader in Danzig, who quit the party and became a fierce critic of Nazism in 1935.

Black, in his 1938 book, *If I Were a Jew*, describes Hitler's attitude toward Christianity: "It is apparent on all sides that since his rise to power there has been a persistent and deliberate effort to de-Christianize Germany, and in this process both Catholics and Protestants have been attacked and victimized by the Reich, which offered a substitute for Christianity, the neo-paganism of present-day Germany."[84] William Harman Black was Chairman of the Inter-Faith Movement and a Justice of the New York Supreme Court.

Herman, in this book, *It's Your Souls We Want*, noted that: "Nazi radicals have spent much time and thought on the destruction of the Christian Church, especially since they have come to feel that Christianity is a galling deterrent to the ruthless measures which must be taken if their New World Order is to be realized."[85] Stewart Herman was Pastor of the American Church in Berlin for six years before America entered the Second World War. Herman helped coordinate relief efforts after the war with the World Council of Churches and also helped with refugee services. He was later President of the Lutheran School of Theology in Chicago.

In 1937 Stephen H. Roberts wrote in his book, *The House That Hitler Built*, that the hostility between Nazism and churches began as soon as the Nazis came to power,

---

[82] Herman Rauschning, *The Revolution of Nihilism*, (New York: Alliance Books, 1939), p. 90.

[83] *The Revolution of Nihilism*, Raushning, p. 119.

[84] William Harman Black, *If I Were a Jew*, (New York: Real Book, 1938), p. 267.

[85] *It's Your Souls We Want*, Herman, p. 48.

and that it quickly became impossible to be a good Catholic and a good Nazi. Some Nazis were overtly and clearly anti-Christian. Others were simply silent. Hitler, however, did nothing to stop the drumbeat of pagan propaganda within the Nazi Party which included Heinrich Himmler, Baldur von Schirach, Alfred Rosenberg, Dr. Frick and many others, some of whom formally renounced their Christianity. The Confessional groups of Christians - Protestants who had refused to join the "German Christian" movement - sent Hitler a letter in May 1936 asking whether he intended to "de-Christianize the German people." The response was wholly unsatisfactory, with the Christian clergy believing that Hitler had accepted "honors due only to God."[86] Stephen Roberts was a professor of History at the University of Sydney and the author of many books on the history of Europe and Australia.

Dorothy Thompson wrote on October 17, 1938 that National Socialism, like Communism, was a secular religion and that until that was understood, then nothing about Nazism and Communism made sense. She then noted that both violated the First Commandment, "Thou shalt have no other gods before Me." Then Thompson states that this is why the most formidable opposition to both these totalitarianism movements came from people of faith; and that while it may be possible to unite Communism or National Socialism with some economic theory or political system or sociology, it is absolutely impossible to harmonize either with the Bible. She observes that those who have thrown their lot with Hitler in Germany were those without serious religious convictions, and that Hitler has found the only opponent he could not terrorize or bribe among the Christians of Germany.[87] Thompson was the first journalist to

---

[86] Henry Wolfe, *The German Octopus*, (New York: Doubleday, 1938), p. 18.

[87] *Let the Record Speak*, Thompson, pp. 239 – 240.

be thrown out of Nazi Germany, and in 1939 she was considered by *Time Magazine* to be one of the two most influential women in America.

In 1939, Ogg wrote in *European Government and Politics* that from the Nazi viewpoint Christianity was part of the common value systems which the Nazis most vigorously opposed, that the Nazis specifically objected to values of "a common European origin" and that Nazism opposed reason as a workable guide to social action.[88] Frederick Austen Ogg was a professor at several American universities and the author or co-author of seventeen books. He was in 1941 the President of the American Political Science Association.

In 1941, in *Ridde of the Reich*, Wythe and Parry state: "Christ stands for love, forgiveness, tolerance, equality. For these Nazis have no stomach."[89] Andrew Parry was editorial and research director of the American Council Against Nazi Propaganda, founded by Professor William Dodd, Ambassador to Germany.

In 1938 Hendrik Willem van Loon stated that Hitler has tried to deprive society of the only foundation on which true civilization and world peace can be grounded, Christianity, and for that van Loon leaves Hitler to the judgment of God.[90] Hendrik Willen van Loon was an internationally recognized author, who had thirty published books, including the very first Newberry Award in 1927.

In 1940, M.W. Fodor, in his book, *The Revolution is On!* writes that "National Socialism also revived the persecution of the churches, surpassing all other revolutions in its anti-clerical attitude. The 'godless' in Russia have enormous organization, but there were only a few instances

---

[88] *European Government and Politics*, Ogg, p. 730.
[89] *Riddle of the Reich*, Wythe and Parry, p. 142.
[90] Henrik van Loon, *Our Battle*, (New York: Simon & Schuster, 1938), p. 131.

of organized violation of the sanctity of the churches. In Germany not only Christians but Christianity is being persecuted."[91] Fodor was an internationally respected journalist who knew Trotsky and many of the key figures of the first half of the last century and who wrote books warning of the dangers of Nazism.

I have cited twenty books, all written during the years in which the Nazis were in power and all concluding that the Nazis were hostile to Christianity. I could easily have cited more books. The authors of these books came from a wide variety of backgrounds. Several were Jewish. Others were professors. Many were famous authors and journalists. These twenty authors are also all respected and distinguished individuals – several, like Jacob Marcus, Dorothy Thompson, Frederick Ogg, Hendrik Willem van Loon, Stewart Herman, William Harman Black and Max Weinrich would be considered the authoritative source for many world issues. And they all agree about Nazis animus toward Christianity.

Why did I cite so many sources? Because, in spite of what so many serious and knowledgeable authors were writing about Nazi antipathy toward Christianity, there will always be people who dislike or hate Christianity and who, therefore, will latch onto whatever they can to try to link Christianity to Nazism. When we consider in later chapters what the Nazis did to Christians and how Christians, alone, openly resisted the Nazis, the proposition that Nazism was the product of Christianity becomes untenable.

---

[91]   M.W. Foder, *The Revolution is On!* (Boston: Houghton Mifflin, 1940), p. 223.

Chapter 4
The Nazi War on Christians

The persecution of Christians, unlike that of Jews, was not publicized to the outside world, as Power notes (italics in original): *"Both Hitler and the Party still maintain – at any rate in all statements made for foreign consumption – that there has been at no time any persecution of religion in the Reich."*[92] And Power goes on to express his own opinion: "Inside Germany there has not been much attempt to pretend that the Church was anything but a thorn in the side of the State, to be treated in a language that could only be used upon a persecuted people."[93] Inside Germany the Nazis treated Christians like a persecuted people, but the Nazis lied about how they treated Christians to the rest of the world.

The destruction of Christians would also come after the destruction of Jews, as Myers noted in his book: "The concerted move to dispose of Christianity did not come until after the Jews had been crushed, or well-nigh so. Then to damn Christianity in the eyes of a people already crazed against the Jews, Nazi writers set about railing against it as nothing more than a Jewish product."[94]

---

[92]   *Religion in the Reich*, Power, p. 225.
[93]   *Religion in the Reich*, Power, p. 226.
[94]   *The History of Bigotry in America*, Myers, p. 388.

The actions of the Nazis against Christianity were manifest in the early actions of the Nazis. The New Standard Encyclopedia of 1934, scarcely after the Nazis had come to power, noted that "attacks on the clergy and suppression of Catholic organs was frequent."[95] Krzeniski writes that when they came to power "The Nazis became increasingly bold. Passive opposition became less frequent, since more and more to it had to be atoned for in blood, in prison sentences, beatings and confinement in concentration camps. The iron hand of Nazidom came down heavily upon both Catholics and Protestants."[96] From the beginning of Nazi rule, churchmen were subject to physical violence and imprisonment.

This is also what Williams and Parry relate in their 1941 book, *Riddle of the Reich*, when writing about the Nazi approach to Catholic groups: "From the very first year of the Nazi regime, carefully planned restrictions were applied to such educational and welfare organizations as the Catholic Library Association with its 5,500 branches, the Seaman's Union, the St. Vincent and the St. Boniface Societies, the Catholic student groups and apprentices' homes, and many other institutions."[97]

What happened to Catholics happened to Protestants: The Deutsche Christen, or "German Christian" movement sponsored by the Nazis quickly evolved into a movement to oppress real Christianity, as Power wrote concerning early 1933: "Not long later the state seized the opportunity to appoint a Dr. Jaeger, a fervent follower of the Deutsche Christen, as head of the Evangelical Church in Prussia 'to restore order.' This he did by importing numbers of secret police and arresting a number of pastors."[98] In Prussia, the

---

[95] *If I Were a Jew*, Black, p. 115.
[96] *National Cultures, Nazism and the Church*, Krzeninski, p. 68.
[97] *Riddle of the Reich*, Wythe, p. 117.
[98] *Religion in the Reich*, Power, p. 112.

largest state by far in Germany, the Nazi response to serious Christians was almost from the beginning to call in the Gestapo.

The Nazis moved violently against Christianity during its very first year in power. They attacked the Catholic Church. They sent the secret police to arrest Protestant ministers in Prussia. But Nazi leaders were not content with simple violent intimidation. They added personal contempt, and this showed up in calculated snubs: "On March 21 [1933], as if for the benefit of any Catholic still uncertain as to the official attitude to the Church, Hitler and Goebbels publicly refused to attend the solemn opening of Mass at Potsdam. They were careful to underline this by giving as their reason that they considered it more important to lay wreaths on the tombs of the S.A. men in Berlin."[99] Hitler and Goebbels, two Nazis who had at least a hypothetical Christianity, still went out of their way within weeks of the Nazis taking power to show their disdain for Christian practices.

During his same first year: "On June 11, one of the two great Catholic Workers Unions, the Catholic Journeymen's Association, were addressed in Munich by von Papen. The Vice-Chancellor appealed to them to co-operate in building up the new order. But they received little immediate encouragement, for they were set upon the moment they left the hall. Priests accompanying them were beaten with steel and rubber truncheons."[100] Again, overt violence against Christians appeared when the Nazis had been in power less than a year. The war on Christianity – the real and violent war – began even before Hitler was president of Germany; even while Hindenburg, who was not hostile to Christianity, still had the power to oust Hitler or dismiss him as chancellor or rouse the army against him, still Hitler could

---

[99] *Religion in the Reich*, Power, p. 28.
[100] *Religion in the Reich*, Power, p. 41.

not refrain from terrorizing Christians.

On September 5, 1933, at a meeting of the General Synod of the Evangelical Church of Prussia, the Reichsbishop threatened anyone who "spread false information abroad" with internment in a concentration camp.[101] This fit in with the Nazi pattern of lying to the world about how the Nazis really felt about Christians and Christianity. How odd that people today, who recognize the great evil of Nazism, take the Nazis at their word when the Nazis are quoted as saying, from time to time, that they have no problem with Christianity.

The next year, in 1934, the Nazis ratcheted up their pressure. On January 11, the Prussian secret police broke into the homes of members of the Pastors Emergency Federation in Berlin, Dortmund and Stettin, confiscated memberships lists, and sent Pastor Rzadki to a concentration camp.[102] On January 22, 1934, the Nazis broke into the study of Dr. Jacobi, a major Protestant church leader who opposed the Nazis, and beat him up.[103] On February 7, Nazi Bishop Muller promulgated a decree which allowed him to transfer pastors from one parish to another or to retire them at will.[104]

Soon thereafter "All 'public meetings' of Catholics were forbidden by General Goering, who asserted that assembly inside churches must suffice. In May, 1934, this was being carried out even in the Saar territory, where promises once made by the Nazis could now be broken with impunity."[105] And on the Night of the Long Knives: "On June 30...in the blood-bath that shocked the whole

---

[101] *The Struggle for Religious Freedom in Germany,* Duncan-Jones, p. 50.

[102] *God among the Germans,* Douglass, p. 235.

[103] *The Struggle for Religious Freedom in Germany,* Duncan-Jones, p. 72.

[104] *God among the Germans,* Douglass, p. 239.

[105] *Like a Mighty Army,* Schuster, p. 257.

world, a Dr. Klausener was among those assassinated on Hitler's orders. Dr. Klausener was the head of Catholic Action in Berlin."[106] Adalbert Probst, the head of the Catholic Youth Sports Association, was also murdered by the Nazis at the same time as was Fritz Gerlich, a leading Catholic publisher.

In October 1934, Dr. Wurm, a leader of the Confessional Church, was placed under house arrest with police outside his home day and night. About the same time, Nazi religious hack Jaeger appeared in church offices in Munich with the Gestapo. He locked the doors of the church, confiscated the organ and church papers, and announced that he was deposing Dr. Meiser, a Christian leader.[107]

On March 14, 1935, the Nazis arrested or put under house arrest 700 pastors for reading the manifesto of the Provisional Church (another name for the Confessional Church) which denounced Nazi racism. Another 5,000 pastors were visited by the Gestapo.[108] Soon after that, as the Dean of Chichester observed: "The determination of the pastors to read the manifesto remained unbroken, with the consequence that a wave of arrests followed. The concentration camp was now used more freely, instead of mere house arrest or confinement for a few days."[109]

The persecution of the Catholic press grew even tighter: "Since the Amann decrees of April 24, 1935 – 'measures taken for the safeguarding of the daily press' – one thousand newspapers have been put down, and hundreds of others have been forced to cease publication through the dismissal of their staff. Those papers that remained,

---

[106] *Religion in the Reich*, Power, p. 48.

[107] *The Struggle for Religious Freedom in Germany*, Duncan-Jones, pp. 88-89.

[108] *The Struggle for Religious Freedom in Germany*, Duncan-Jones, p. 100.

[109] *The Struggle for Religious Freedom in Germany*, Duncan-Jones, p. 101.

whether with a Catholic tradition or without it, were bound by law to carry all Party speeches and forbidden any form of criticism."[110]

By August 1935, the persecution of Christianity was so common that Schuster wrote: "Jail sentences and attacks on individuals are no longer anything new. But the systematic attack on every religious institution could only mean that Germany had definitely become an anti-Christian government; and the wholesale desecration of churches and shrines; often in ways unspeakably vile, indicated clearly that the Nazi Party harbored large elements between whom and the godless of Russia was no discernible difference."[111]

What sorts of things did Christian clergy endure early in the Nazi regime? In 1935, Schuster wrote: "Recourse was had to a veritable reign of terror, the history of which cannot yet be written. Throughout Germany, orthodox pastors and their congregations were harassed by secret police and bands of S.A. Even funeral processions were broken up, and violence was witnessed even in the very houses of worship."[112]

On December 2, 1935, Kerrl forbade any church association from appointing pastors, from examining theological candidates, from inspecting parishes, from issuing instructions or announcements from the pulpit, from collecting funds for administrative purposes or from summoning Synods.[113]

Black wrote that: "...The Reich has not limited its anti-Christianity to official pronouncements. Schools, hospitals, and other institutions of the Church are being confiscated; a 'religious' instruction based on Germanic neo-paganism is being introduced; and the elimination of Christian influence

---

[110] *Religion in the Reich*, Power, p. 75.
[111] *Like a Mighty Army*, Schuster, p. 271.
[112] *Like a Mighty Army*, Schuster, p. 123.
[113] *The Struggle for Religious Freedom in Germany*, Duncan-Jones,, p. 130.

from the education of the youth, and from the cultural life of the German people is continuing apace. In February, 1936, nearly all the leaders of the Catholic Young Men's Association of Germany were arrested on the charge of having organized in cooperation with the Communist Party a secret plot against Hitler."[114]

Nazis tried to hide their persecution of Christians because it would complicate their relationships with other nations. Nevertheless, when the pastor of the American Church in Berlin was invited to a Nazi Party luncheon in 1936, he came with the understanding that he could say a prayer. He relates the following: "Everyone looked somewhat startled when it was announced that grace would be said. Apparently they were even more startled at the nature of that little prayer, which obtained a temporary niche in history when Louis Lochner sent an account of it to New York as the first Christian prayers offered at an official Nazi function. It was probably the last."[115]

In another book, Herman wrote: "On April 17, 1936, Hitler's deputy, Rudolph Hess, forbade any Party official to occupy a church position. In June the sale of the Bible and the rental of rooms for religions purposes were stopped. The Reich Minister of Education, Rust, prohibited university students from taking sides in the confessional struggle. Leading personages in the Party and state left the church in increasing numbers. It was no longer a secret that the Party exercised strong pressure on all its members, especially on the state employees and members of the S.S., the police, and the youth organizations which now belonged completely to the state. Everyone who desired to get a good position was obliged to resign from the church."[116]

By July, 1936, a manifesto was read in thousands of

---

[114] *If I Were a Jew*, Black, p. 268.
[115] *It's Your Souls We Want*, Herman, p. ix.
[116] *The Rebirth of the German Church*, Herman, p. 41.

churches in Germany, which said: "Things have come to such a pass that the honor of German citizens is being dragged through the mud because they are Christians. The Christian population of Germany note with strong emotion and indignation that they are jeered at and mocked at in every way (press, theatre, lectures, mass meetings) because of their faith in Jesus Christ, and the question is asked whether they are reliable. Those who firmly cling to the Gospel are specially suspected in these respects."[117] This was the sort of argument which was regularly waged against German Jews as well: German Jews who had proved themselves in the First World War, who professed their patriotism in every way, even who had originally supported Hitler, all were forever suspect because of their being Jewish. It was exactly the same thing with Christians, except that Christians who renounced Christianity and embraced Nazi paganism were safe. By this time, even collections to help the families of pastors who had been sent to prison or concentration camps were forbidden, and the Gestapo seized any money collected for that purpose.[118]

On November 4, 1936, the Nazis ordered the removal of crucifixes from schools in the Oldenburg area on the grounds that these were "symbols of superstition." This order was rescinded only after Nazis were faced with determined local opposition. Then, in what would become a typical practice, despite rescinding the Nazi prohibition of these "symbols of superstition," in December 1936 Nazi bureaucrats simply removed crucifixes anyway in Munsterland. When Christians replaced them in some schools, they were arrested by the Nazis.[119]

---

[117] *The Struggle for Religious Freedom in Germany*, Duncan-Jones, p. 135.

[118] *The Struggle for Religious Freedom in Germany*, Duncan-Jones, p. 145-146.

[119] Terrence Prittie, *Germans Against Hitler* (Boston: Little, Brown & Company, 1964), pp. 74 – 81.

By 1937, the level of persecution was such that: "Both Catholics and Protestants resisted totalitarian control, and both these groups were violently repressed. In June, 1937, the Prussian Courts ruled that they could not protect either of them against secret police interference. The clergy of both denominations were threatened with prosecution for treason if they sought foreign sympathy. A deputy Nazi party leader barred both Protestants and Catholics from membership."[120]

The same year Herman wrote: "Cold-bloodedly the government went on issuing decrees and making arrests until virtually the whole leadership of the Confessional Church was put behind bars as common criminals"[121] and Black, describing the same oppression, wrote: "During April, May and June arrest followed arrest. The Gestapo broke into houses, stole documents, impounded pastors. By the end of October it is estimated (exact figures are hard to find) that 500 pastors had been arrested."[122]

When the confessional Church openly decried the tenets of the German Christians: "This was too much. The State struck. Seven hundred pastors, including Pastor Neimoller, were arrested and 5,000 others received visits from the Gestapo telling them exactly where they (and the State) stood."[123] After this: "Prayers were offered up in the churches for those pastors who were still in gaol. For the first time congregations learnt that their pastors were being introduced to the rigors of the Concentration Camp."[124]

By December 1937, a Memorandum issued by the Protestant chaplains in the German Army stated: "The new breach which divides the German people, it says 'is the breach between National-Socialism and Christianity.' This

---

[120] *If I Were a Jew*, Black, p. 125.
[121] *It's Your Souls We Want*, Herman, p. 165.
[122] *Religion in the Reich*, Power, pp. 141-142.
[123] *Religion in the Reich*, Power, p. 132.
[124] *Religion in the Reich*, Power, p. 133.

fact is repeatedly denied. It is true nonetheless...In the training camps of the Party it is repeatedly explained that National-Socialism has three enemies: Judaism, Masonry and Christianity. Public acceptance of Christianity is regarded, when a new position is filled, as a tie that unfits the candidate for service to the State or Party...The means by which this combat is carried on is the ruthless use of State power...The racial ethic, represented through the Party and the police, armed with all the force of the Totalitarian State, hurls itself against materially helpless Christianity. The situation has become wholly intolerable through the fashion in which State forces are employed...In Halle, a high functionary of the Storm Troops referred to Christ as 'that swine.' School teachers have repeatedly referred to Jesus in their classrooms as 'that Jewish tramp.'"[125]

By 1938, things had gotten so bad that Duncan-Jones wrote: "No effort has been spared to render the Confessional Movement impotent. Its colleges have been suppressed; it funds have been seized; its leaders have been imprisoned over and over again. In the early part of 1938 an attempt was made to sterilize its leadership by orders forbidding the members of the Provisional Church Administration to meet. At the time of writing the Confessional Movement is severely smitten. But it carries on, not knowing what may be in store for it, not expecting earthly success, and yet prepared to suffer all that must come, because its strength is not of this world. The resistance of the Confessionals is one of the many great vindications of the indomitable power of conscience that history affords."[126]

Preaching from the pulpit against Rosenberg's racial theories was forbidden by the Nazis and Law 130 threatened penalties against any priest who preached "against the

---

[125] *Religion in the Reich*, Power, pp. 228-229.
[126] *The Struggle for Religious Freedom in Germany*, Duncan-Jones, p. 146.

interest of the state." By September 1938, Rosenberg was able to say: "There are hot-heads among us who would like to compel the Fuhrer to simply root out the Catholic and Protestant Churches, just as we have the Bolshevik Party. But...we must remember that the international position of the Catholic Church calls for very careful tactics on our part toward that Church. That the Catholic Church and also the Confessional Church, in their present form, must disappear from the life of the people, is my full conviction, and I believe I am entitled to say that this is also our Fuhrer's viewpoint."[127]

William Harman Black wrote about the months that followed: "While realizing the impossibility of coordinating the Catholic Church with the Nazi regime, the Nazis followed a policy of restricting Catholic activities, of discrediting the Church with the German people, and of extending their control over Catholic youth"[128] and "Orders from Berlin then forbade opposition pastors to speak in public, placed their churches under lock and key, and caused the arrest of Bishop Wurm, and many of his followers. Meanwhile Mueller toured Wurttenberg, speaking chiefly at gatherings recruited by the S.A. and asserting categorically that the Church would either embrace National Socialism or cease to be."[129] Half the members of monasteries had been arrested by 1938.[130] By 1938 religious radio broadcasts were completely banned, and two years after that religious publications were banned as well (allegedly on the grounds of paper shortages.)[131]

By 1938, Dark and Essex wrote: "It has been forbidden to have collecting boxes in church rooms or even in Evangelical homes. The publication of church news has been

---

[127] *Religion in the Reich*, Power, pp. 173-174.
[128] *If I Were a Jew*, Black, p. 118.
[129] *Like a Mighty Army*, Schuster, p. 142
[130] *If I Were a Jew*, Black, p. 269.
[131] *It's Your Souls We Want*, Herman, pp. 183-184.

much curtailed by legislation, which enacts that all editors must be members of the National Press Association, which requires that its member shall be ready to answer accusations against 'political reliability.' If their explanation is not considered satisfactory, they are expelled from the Association and this means that they can carry on their work no longer. Church papers, parish magazines and other church literature have been brought to a complete standstill. There was an attempt soon after these regulations were introduced to institute a news service by means of duplicating machines, but as soon as this scheme was made known, the duplicators were confiscated."[132] The steadily increasing persecution of Christianity and Christians ratcheted up each month and each year, much like the Nazi persecution of Jews: it became more and more difficult to be a Christian in Nazi Germany.

Describing the 1938 takeover of Austria by the Nazis, Power writes: "All over Austria men and women have lost their jobs for professing openly their faith. The Party has never attempted to conceal the fact that only its own members stand a good chance of obtaining the best positions in civil employment. Sometimes there has even been a 'drive' against Catholics in a business, and all those who refused to sign the form by which they are given the chance to deny the Church, dismissed. In one of the great Vienna hospitals where Catholic nursing sisters have worked for years, the entire staff was thrown out and their places taken over by National-Socialist 'Brown Sisters.'"[133] When the Nazis occupied Austria, they seized the monasteries and convents, sending those nuns and monks who did not escape to concentration camps.[134]

By 1939, Lichtenberger was writing: "In reply to what

---

[132]   *The War Against God*, Dark, p. 188-189.
[133]   *Religion in the Reich*, Power, p. 211.
[134]   *The History of Bigotry in America*, Myers, p. 390.

they consider to be 'provocations,' the National Socialists have multiplied the trials for abuse of the pulpit, they have muzzled the Catholic press, censored or stopped bishops' letters, even suspending the little weekly or diocesan religious bulletins. In the Catholic world information has come to depend on typewritten sheets which circulate under cover or on oral communication by trusted emissaries."[135] The same year, Pierre van Paassen wrote in his book, *Days of Our Lives*, that Germany is farther on the road to dechristianization than the Soviet Union and that in place of God, Nazis have placed the almighty state which demands everything from man.[136] The same year, Ernest Hambloch wrote that because the Roman Catholic Church had been opposing the Nazis as pagan, the Nazis accused the Vatican of being in league with Communism.[137]

By a decree of October 31, 1940, all clergymen had to sign in with the local police office.[138] Christian clergy were also conscripted into military service, not as clergy, but as front line soldiers and they were deliberately sent to the front lines of battle were the mortality rate was the highest.[139] "The Nazi newspaper, *Das Schwarze Korps*, wrote that the German soldiers did not want to be blessed by priests, 'those wretched creatures of dirt and fire,' those representatives of 'pious cowardice.'"[140]

Fodor, who personally knew Russian Bolsheviks and followed closely the Bolshevik Revolution as well as the National Socialist revolution and the Fascist regime, noted

[135] *The Third Reich*, Lichtenberger, p. 210.
[136] Pierre van Paassan, *Days of Our Lives*, (New York: Hillman-Curl, 1939), p. 170.
[137] Ernst Hamloch, *Germany Rampant*, (New York: Carrick & Evans, 1939), p. 82.
[138] *The Rebirth of the German Church*, Herman, p. 46.
[139] Hans Rothfels, *German Opposition to Hitler*, (Hinsdale, IL: Regnery, 1948), p. 44.
[140] *Riddle of the Reich*, Wythe, p. 141.

in his 1940 book that the Nazis surpassed all other totalitarian systems in its persecution of churches, finding even the Soviet Union less hateful toward Christianity than the Nazis, who persecuted not only Christians but Christianity itself.[141]

Churches were not allowed to collect funds for charitable work. The Nazis transferred Catholic clergy to Protestant areas and Protestant clergy to Catholic areas. Nazis smeared excrement on church altars and church doors, desecrated shrines, and threw statutes of saints into dung piles; and when synagogues were not available to attack and loot, churches were often the target with Nazis yelling: "Down with Christians and Jews!" In many places, historic church feast days and holidays were banned and even the display of religious flags and banners was outlawed; often Nazis cordoned off areas necessary for church pilgrimages and offered free beer and sausages for secular events that deliberately coincided with church festivals.[142]

Nazi hatred of Christianity led to the Nazis ruthlessly removing Christianity from public life. "Films are likewise scrupulously irreligious. Even the Spanish film *Alcazar* which glorified the Franco cause was censored and purged of every reference to prayer or faith or God."[143] And Herman, who lived six years in Nazi Germany, observed: "In all my six years in Germany I never saw an impartial, to say nothing of favorable, article on Christianity, unless the annual notice that church taxes were due might be considered impartial."[144] Censorship and thought control in Nazi Germany did not even allow a favorable word about Christianity during the six years in which Herman was in Berlin. Films had pious allusions to Christianity removed. The pat-

---

[141] *The Revolution is On!*, Fodor, p. 223.
[142] *The Third Reich: A New History*, Burleigh, pp. 236 – 261.
[143] *It's Your Souls We Want*, Herman, p. 52.
[144] *It's Your Souls We Want*, Herman, p. 93.

tern was clear: Nazis were intent on assiduously purging German society of the very idea of Christianity.

Black commented on the overall pattern of Nazi actions: "It is apparent on all sides that since his rise to power there has been a persistent and deliberate effort to de-Christianize Germany, and in this process both Catholics and Protestants have been attacked and victimized by the Reich, which offered as a substitute for Christianity the neo-paganism of present-day Germany."[145]

Wythe wrote in 1941 that: "Although not many anti-religious books and pamphlets have been printed by the Nazis since September, 1939, the previously issued literature continues to be plentiful. It is distributed among soldiers and civilians as before. There are brochures of Rudolph Hammer, published in Munich, quoting a certain renegade, Pastor Alfred Bonn, to the effect that Jesus was begot 'in blood shame,' and that his Mother was a woman of easy virtue (a stronger word is used.)"[146]

How marginalized had Christians become in Nazi Germany? Consider that by 1941 all religious education was banned from schools, bands were even forbidden to play chorale music, and even pastoral care in hospitals was being made more and more difficult.[147] "Hotels, or hospices, run by Christian organizations were told to remove all religious pictures from the rooms and Bibles from bedside tables."[148] In June 1941: "It was about this time that pastors were refused admittance to hospitals and clinics unless they came at the written invitation of a patient and with the approval of medical authorities. In such cases they were forbidden to visit or speak to any other invalid."[149]

In his 1941 book, *Pattern of Conquest*, Joseph Harsch

---

[145] *If I Were a Jew*, Black, p. 267.
[146] *Riddle of the Reich*, Wythe, p. 141.
[147] *Christian Counter-Attack*, Martin et al., p.39.
[148] *It's Your Souls We Want*, Herman, p. 218.
[149] *It's Your Souls We Want*, Herman, p. 218.

wrote that Nazism was profoundly anti-Christian and hostile to Western Civilization as well.[150] In 1941, Lowenstein wrote that the Nazis were not content to simply subjugate the churches, but to de-Christianize religion altogether, and to root out "Jewish-Christian" morality.[151]

Albert Parry notes in his 1941 book, *Riddle of the Reich,* that not a single pastoral letter had been permitted by the Nazi government to be read from the pulpit for the three preceding years, and that this ban included even the Pope's encyclicals. Parry goes on to note that Pope Pius XI had protested Nazism, and that the Nazi obituary for Pius XI said that he had began as a Pope but ended as a political adventurer. It went on to say that in the next pope, Pope Pius XII, the German government hoped to find a more pliable personality, but the hope was not fulfilled.[152]

The 1943 book, *Christian Counter-Attack: Europe's Churches Against Nazism,* observes: "Beyond all question the Nazis are waging war upon the Christian faith and Christian values"[153] and the uniqueness of Christian opposition to the Nazis: "While in Germany the political parties, the law, the universities, the Press, the trade unions capitulated, the first check to the triumphant onward march of Nazism was given by a small resolute body of Christian men – the Confessional Church."[154] The same year, Clara Eastlake wrote: "As Germany sees victory slipping from her grasp, she has reinforced the power of the Gestapo and increased the torture, slaughter and wholesale massacre of Christians as well as Jews in her midst."[155]

---

[150] Joseph Harsch, *Patterns of Conquest* (Garden City, NY: Doubleday, Doran and Co., 1941) p. 135.
[151] Karl Lowenstein, *Governments of Continental Europe,* (New York: Macmillan, 1941), p. 549.
[152] *Riddle of the Reich,* Williams and Parry, pp. 133 – 142.
[153] *Christian Counter-Attack,* Martin et al., p. 12.
[154] *Christian Counter-Attack,* Martin et al., p. 15.
[155] *The War Against God,* Carmer, p. 48.

The Nazis entered their reign hostile to Christianity, and although they sometimes tried to mask that animus from the outside world for political reasons, this hatred became real persecution almost as soon as Hitler came to power. Although those who maliciously intend to somehow weave the threads of Christianity through the evil of Nazism may find, here and there, exceptions to the rule (anyone can always find exceptions to the rule), consider that thoughtful critics of Nazism at the time were universal in their general perception: Nazis hated Christianity, persecuted Christianity and considered Christianity – in many ways – the greatest enemy of Nazism.

This chapter covers only the general persecution of Christianity. Perhaps more telling was the war that the Nazis waged upon Christian education of the young. What happened to Christian clergymen was, in some ways, irrelevant to Nazis. Drown a couple of generations in loathing for Judeo-Christianity. The "Judeo" part was easy from the venom reserved for Nazis against Jews; less know, but critically important, was the Nazi venom spent on Christians.

Chapter 5
The Nazi War on Christian Education

The Nazis conducted a systematic effort to keep children from learning or practicing Christianity, as Herman saw while he was in Germany: "Children were encouraged to abandon the religious classes and teachers were prohibited from continuing the lessons. Only clergymen were allowed to teach religion whereby a further reduction of the number of classes became inevitable. When Wurrtemberg clergymen refused to teach religion according to the illegal instructions of the Ministry of Education, 700 clergymen were banned from classes. This arbitrary measure was founded on the assertion that these resisting clergymen had violated the oath sworn to Hitler! The lessons of religion were entirely suppressed in many districts. Also Christian prayers were abolished in schools and crucifixes were removed from rooms."[156] It was not so much that religion was banned in German schools as it was that Christianity was banned in German schools.

The Nazi War on Christian education moved at least as fast as the Nazi War on Christian churches. By 1935 it had reached the point, according to Schuster, that: "Catholic parents viewed with profound alarm the virtual segregation

---

[156] *The Rebirth of the German Church*, Herman, pp. 44-45.

of their children. Statements that henceforth the civil service would be recruited solely from those who had belonged to the *Hitlerjugend* were followed by other equally discriminatory pronouncements"[157] and "In order to make the situation more difficult still, Baldur von Shirach issued a regulation prohibiting simultaneous membership in both Catholic and Nazi organizations. Various business enterprises in quest of government contracts then also began to discriminate against youthful employees not identified with Hitler groups."[158] The Nazi efforts were not just directed against Christian education but against parents and students who sought Christian education. Preventing civil service advancement to young people who had Christian instruction and pressuring businesses not to hire young people who had Christian instruction was the sort of bigotry toward Christianity which did not occur outside the Soviet Union.

The same year, 1935, the Nazis attacked Christian schools themselves, as Power states: "These placards, on walls, on houses and telegraph poles, proclaimed: 'One People, One Reich, One Fuhrer – One Community School' 'He who sends his child to the denominational school, wrongs his child – and interferes with the unity of our people,' 'We do not want Catholic or Evangelical schools, we want the school of Adolph Hitler.'"[159]

The harassment of Christian youth, particularly Catholic youth, was appalling. During the same year, 1935, Power also tells of the mistreatment of Catholic youth in a particular incident: "The length to which the State was prepared to go is best shown by the case of the two thousand Catholic boys who paid a visit to the Holy Father in Rome at Easter, 1935. On their return from the audience which

---

[157] *Like a Mighty Army,* Schuster, p.210.
[158] *Like a Mighty Army,* Schuster, p. 211.
[159] *Religion in the Reich*, Power, p. 51.

they were granted they were set upon at the frontier, at Constance, by the secret police. Their cameras, rucksacks, rosaries, musical instruments, souvenirs of Rome – everything they had with them was confiscated. Their shirts were torn off their backs. They did not see their belongings again."[160] The same year, Catholic girls out on an excursion in Weiden in the Oberplaz were attacked by Hitler Youth, thrown to the ground and beaten black and blue.[161] The same year, Hoelz, an adjutant to Julius Streicher, said at Nuremberg: "Instead of running to church with your mothers you ought to stay at home and prepare food for your fathers. And when somebody will send you boys to Divine Service you had better play football."[162]

Schuster writes of the end of 1935: "On December 8th he [Mueller] startled Germany by arbitrarily declaring that henceforth the Evangelical youth groups would be incorporated into the *Hitlerjugend*. This was an exceedingly sore point with the opposition because Baldur von Shirach, leader of the *Hitlerjugend*, was an outspoken pagan who declared that belief in Germany must take precedence over allegiance to any church."[163] In fact, as a part of the initiation into the Hitler Youth, boys were required to state: "German blood and Christian baptismal water are completely irreconcilable."[164]

By 1936, the situation grew worse for those who wanted their children to be involved in Christian youth activities: "In 1936, further encroachments were made by the Hitler youth on the Catholic organizations. Youth members were forbidden to wear the XP badges, and bands, uniforms and flags were prohibited for public processions

---

[160] *Religion in the Reich*, Power, p. 58.
[161] *The Struggle for Religious Freedom in Germany*, Duncan-Jones, p. 172.
[162] *The War Against God*, Carmer, p. 11.
[163] *Like a Mighty Army*, Schuster, pp. 116-117.
[164] *Nazism versus Religion*, Freely, p. 22.

or group formation."[165]

Himmler banned all Confessing Church seminaries and instruction in 1937 and he closed all private religious schools two years later. Parents and children were made hostage to poverty if children received a Christian education, and Power writes that: "It was made clear, over and over again, that to vote for the Confessional school was to vote treacherously and against the new Germany, and against the express wishes of the Fuhrer himself. More important still to parents of large and often poor families, it was made increasingly clear that only children at the community school enjoyed the best changes of work when their education was complete."[166] The Nazis intimidated people by whatever devices they had to reject a Christian education.

So what happened when children entered the Hitler Youth? Did this Nazi organization accept Christianity? Was it indifferent toward Christianity? Or was it hostile to Christianity? Consider the inscription over the clinic at the Hitler Youth center at Halle: "The Faith fanatics, who still to-day slide down on their knees with faces uplifted to heaven, waste their time in churchgoing and prayers, and have not yet understood that they are living on the earth and that therefore their task is of a thoroughly earthly kind. All we Hitler people can still only look with the greatest contempt on those young people who still run to their silly Evangelical or Catholic Churches in order to vent their quite superstitious religious feelings."[167] Those effectively conscripted in the Hitler Youth were told that ordinary Christians were "faith fanatics" and Protestants and Catholics had "superstitious religious feelings." The Hitler Youth was intended to pound Christianity out of children.

---

[165] *The War Against God*, Dark, p. 202.
[166] *Religion in the Reich*, Power, p. 52.
[167] *Religion in the Reich*, Power, p. 60.

William Harman Black wrote his book in 1938: "The initial battle is for control of the youth of the country. The Christian Church, on the one hand, desires to maintain its parochial schools, where the young people may grow up with an education based on the morals and the manners of the Christian religion; on the other hand, the German State wants to divorce all religion from the education of its youth. As Hitler himself announced 'The State must control all attitude, shaping influences finally, completely and irrevocably.'"[168] This was the heart of the matter. Hitler and the Nazis would not allow anything that provided a different message from Nazism. The voice of conscience which Christian education would give was incompatible with Christianity. It must be ruthlessly purged.

In 1939 Lichtenberger commented on the complete isolation of Catholic youth: "The young Catholic, faithful to his association, is condemned to lead the solitary life of a semi-pariah, happy when he is not treated by his Nazi comrades as a renegade and traitor to Germanism and is not insulted and beaten"[169] and he also noted the Nazification of education in those places in Germany which once had Catholic education: "Uniform Nazis have replaced Catholic priests and professors in higher schools and Catholic nuns in lower schools and kindergartens."[170]

In 1941, when the Nazi tract *Gott und Volk* was distributed, Herman noted how the Nazis intended children to grow up. It describes how the Nazis would replace Christianity so that students would be able to grow up without ever knowing Christianity: "With parties and gifts the youth will be led painlessly from one faith to the other and will grow up without ever having heard of the Sermon on the Mount or the Golden Rule, to say nothing of the Ten

---

[168] *If I Were a Jew*, Black, p. 267.
[169] *The Third Reich*, Lichtenberger, p. 209.
[170] *Riddle of the Reich*, Wythe, p. 137.

Commandments. This goal was openly proclaimed in a book entitled *Gott und Volk* which was distributed in the hundreds of thousands of copies throughout the army in the spring of 1941. In Chapter XIII entitled 'Our Task' there is a paragraph which says, 'The education of the youth is to be confined primarily by the teacher, the officer, and the leaders of the party. The priests will die out. They have estranged the youth from the Volk. Into their places will step the leaders. Not deputies of God. But anyway the best Germans. And how shall we train our children? Thus, as though they had never heard of Christianity!'"[171]

In fact, members of German Christian youth organization were required to resign from those even before joining the *Hitlerjugend*, and as MacFarland writes: "Even if double membership were permitted, the Hitler Youth Movement takes up so large an amount of time and has so attractive an appeal that the religious groups would be weakened in allegiance. Moreover it is claimed that great pressure is brought on the church youth, by their friends in the Hitler movement and in schools, by all sorts of propaganda, to unite with that organization."[172]

What sort of things did the *Hitlerjugend* teach about Christianity? Power reports that the lines handed out to Hitler Youth teaches which he saw included: "Christianity is a religion of slaves and fools." "How did Christ die? Whining at the Cross!" "The Ten Commandments represent the lowest instincts of man." and "Christianity is merely a cloak for Judaism."[173]

Erika Mann, in her book *School for Barbarians*, wrote that the fanatic war of National Socialism against the Church is fought on so large a field that the contest results only in battles won by one side and then the other, but that

[171] *It's Your Souls We Want*, Herman, p. 29.
[172] *The New Church and the New Germany*, MacFarland, p. 161,
[173] *Religion in the Reich*, Power, pp. 175-176.

one thing is clear: "the stake of the war is the souls of the children. Both sides are battling for their future" and that the remedy proposed by the Nazis to solve the enemy of Christianity was to take Christian children, whose parents insisted on teaching them Christian virtues, away from their parents (much like the Bolsheviks would take Christian children away from their parents). Duncan-Jones said almost exactly the same thing in his book: "The school was the sphere where conflict between the Christian faith and the Nazi religion was most acute because the Nazis were determined at all costs to obtain the possession of the souls of the young."[174]

This extended to the "War on Christmas" so familiar in America today. When German youths were evacuated by the government: "One of the chief grounds of complaint, circulated privately if not presented publicly, was the deliberate attempt to wean Christian children away from their religion. They were told not to say their prayers or ask to go to the local church. When Christmas came, parents were horrified to learn that the children's festivities, while elaborate, were shorn of every Christian symbol. In one camp a few homesick kiddies who gathered in one room the day after Christmas began to sing 'Silent Night' and some other carols were severely reprimanded for attempting to augment the German Christmas by the introduction of alien customs."[175]

Lowenstein in 1941 wrote that in the Hitler Youth the neo-pagan cult began to fill the gap which was the result of a conscious erosion of Christianity. The Nazis even forbade parents to give their children Christian names and ordered babies instead to be given names like Dietrich, Otto or Siegfried. The home teaching of Christianity by parents in

---

[174] *The Struggle for Religious Freedom in Germany,* Duncan-Jones, pp. 130-131.
[175] *It's Your Souls We Want,* Herman, pp. 217-218.

the home was forbidden.[176]

Herman noted in his 1943 book: "It remains to be seen whether the faith confessed by the thousands of boys before the Christian altars of Germany or the faith professed by tens of thousands of enthusiastic youngsters in oaths of fidelity to Hitler will prove stronger. There is no longer any doubt that these two faiths exist and that one of them must be destroyed if the other is to exist."[177]

The Nazi war on Christian education was something that was constantly mentioned by authors of books about the Third Reich. There was very little doubt either by the actions and words of the Nazis or by the opinions expressed by many authors that the Nazis intended to de-Christianize Germany by isolating the young of Germany from all Christian influence.

---

[176] *What Hitler Wants*, Lorimer, pp. 146 – 147.
[177] *It's Your Souls We Want*, Herman, pp. xiv-xv.

Chapter 6
The Christian Response to Nazism

Who opposed the Nazis on moral grounds? Who openly resisted the Nazis? The only real opponents that the Nazis had in Germany were Christians. What about the Bolsheviks? Did they not oppose the Nazis? Eugene Lyons in his masterpiece, *The Red Decade*, states: "In the middle of 1931, upon direct orders from Moscow, the German communists voted with the Nazis against the Prussians and against the Republic."[178] In 1931, the Communist Party of Germany cooperated with the Nazi Party in the Prussian referendum.

The next year, as Calvin Hoover notes in his book, *Germany Enters the Third Reich*, Communist and Nazi labor unions joined together to support the general strike of Berlin transportation workers just prior to the November 1932 election, which was a rude shock to conservatives who had assumed that National Socialism meant an end of labor unions and strikes and the delivery of workers to the mercies of the employer.[179]

This need not have been a rude shock. Nazi and Com-

---

[178] Eugene Lyon, *The Red Decade*, (New Rochelle, NY: Arlington House, 1970), reprint of 1941 Bobbs-Merrill, p. 160.

[179] Calvin Hoover, *Germany Enters the Third Reich* (New York: Macmillan, 1934), p. 74.

munist labor unions often collaborated in strikes and by 1931, two years before Hitler was made Chancellor of Germany, Nazi labor unions had more members than Communist labor unions. In 1934, while still only in power a short time, Hitler told Herman Raushning, the Nazi leader of Danzig: "National Socialism is what Marxism might have been if it could have broken its absurd and artificial ties with a democratic order."

Large numbers of German Communists joined the Nazi Party before it came to power.[180] In fact, many Communists, on orders from Moscow, joined the Nazi Party and rose to high positions within the Nazi Party and worked with zeal as Nazis long before the Nazis gained power. German Communists even joined the Nazi Party after Hitler came to power. How did Nazis view non-Jewish German Communists? In his 1936 book, *Government in the Third Reich*, Morstein Marx states that National Socialist attorneys were prohibited from accepting cases from Jews, but told to never refuse a case from any non-Jewish Communist because Communists were merely misled.

Jan Valtain in his 1942 book, *Out of the Night*, describes his career as one of the most important Communists in Germany. The book, published in America while the Soviet Union was an ally of America, described his torture by the Nazis and his complete disillusionment with Bolshevism. It describes in detail the direct collaboration between the Nazi Party and the Communist Party in the 1930s. The Communists, for example, sent a courier to the Nazi Party in the spring of 1932 asking the Nazis to collaborate with them in breaking up the Transport Worker's Union conference and the two groups, Nazis and Communists, did just that. On another occasion the Nazis sent a request to the Communist Party to disrupt Social Democrats and the Communists obliged, sitting side by side with the Nazis in

---

[180] *Germany Enters the Third Reich*, Hoover, p. 134.

the front row before interrupting Paul von Lettow-Vorbeck, yelling obscenities, throwing stink bombs and itching power, and releasing a large number of white mice into the crowds. Georgi Dimitrov, Bulgarian Secretary-General of Comintern, even ordered Communists to vote with Nazis to oust the Social Democrat Party in Prussia, which the Communists did.[181] Vyacheslav Molotov, addressing the Supreme Soviet on October 31, 1939, said that it was criminal to wage a war against Hitlerism disguised as a fight for the democracies. The non-aggression pact of August 23, 1939 was not the only agreement signed between the Nazis and Soviets. They signed a treaty of friendship on September 28, 1939; they signed a comprehensive trade agreement on February 11, 1940; and they signed a supplementary trade agreement on January 10, 1941.

Once the Second World War in Europe actually began, all the Communist parties in Europe blamed Britain and France for starting the war and said Germany wanted peace. The French government banned the Communist Party because of its disloyalty to France in the war with Germany. French Communists opposed rearmament even though France was at war.

Marxist renegade Louis Fischer in 1940 observed that the Bolsheviks and the Nazis were doing everything possible to avoid acts which displeased the other. They actually began defending what the other was doing. Bolsheviks did not merely justify their deeds in Poland, but they defended what the Nazis were doing in Poland as well. *Izvestia* on October 9, 1939 stated "the government of the Soviet Union and the government of Germany undertook the task of establishing peace and order on the territory of the former Poland and to give to the peoples inhabiting that territory a peaceful existence which would correspond to their na-

---

[181]   Jan Valtain, *Out of the Night* (Garden City, NY: Garden City Publishing Company, 1942) pp. 253 -255.

tional characteristics."After the Second World War began, until the German Army invaded the Soviet Union in June, 1941, Bolsheviks were enthusiastic supporters of the Nazis and the Nazis were very careful to say nothing offensive about the Bolsheviks.

What about the other institutions in Germany that might have opposed the Nazis? All of them were completely compromised. Academia was the most easily seduced part of German culture. Martin Heidegger, perhaps the most influential philosopher of the Twentieth Century, joined the Nazi Party and maintained a strong allegiance to the party, serving as one of its leading intellectuals. After the Second World War, Heidegger was defended by Leftists for active support for the Nazi reign.

In 1936 Nazi racial theorist Alfred Ploetz was nominated for the Nobel Peace Prize for his work in racial hygiene.[182] Konrad Lorenz, the brilliant behavioral psychologist whose theory of imprinting was demonstrated when he convinced ducklings that he was their mother and whose work is profoundly influential today was, like Heidegger, not simply a camp following of Nazism and Hitler but an enthusiastic supporter of National Socialism and of Adolph Hitler.

University students were particularly susceptible to Nazism and by 1930, three years before the Nazis gained power, the National Socialist Student Association or NSDStD was the most popular student association on the college campuses of Germany. These were the very college campuses that were turning out the world's leading physicists and the world's most respected philosophers and intellectuals of every stripe.

The only people who openly opposed the Nazis and who continued to oppose the Nazis were serious Christians.

---

[182] Kristie Macrakis, *Surviving the Swastika* (Oxford, England: Oxford University Press, 1993), pp. 97 – 111.

When the eight bishops of Bavaria met in February 1931, they said: "The Church must conclude that what National Socialism calls Christianity is not the Christianity of Christ."[183] These bishops issued a declaration that protested against Nazi racial policies and forbade priests to give the sacraments to any members of the Nazi Party.[184]

Otto Debelius, the General Superintendent of the Mark of Brandenburg, in early 1933 responded to Nazi hate by stating: "We are united in affirming that the Gospel stands in opposition to all human ideology, whether nationalist or socialist."[185] In December of that year, Catholic Cardinal Faulhaber specifically called upon Protestants and Catholics to make common cause in defense of Christianity and against the paganism of the Nazis.[186] Soon thereafter, the Pastors' Emergency Federation was proclaiming about the Nazi Bishop "He has tried to muzzle us, but we refuse to be muzzled."[187]

In his 1934 book, *The New Church and the New Germany*, Charles MacFarland, writing less than a year after Hitler took power and having interviewed Hitler himself, wrote: "National Socialism in Germany discovered little difficulty in its complete transformation of the life and even the mind of the nation, until it struck the Protestant Christian Church, or more particularly, the pastors of those churches.

At this point it has aroused a near counter-revolution in which, unless the state is cautious, as at last accounts it appears to be, it may meet its Waterloo, by arousing to resistance not a few of the people in general who have thus far

---

[183] *Religion in the Reich*, Power, p. 15.
[184] Ronald Knox, *Nazi and Narazene* (London: MacMillan, 1940), p. 5.
[185] *The Struggle for Religious Freedom in Germany*, Duncan-Jones, p. 36.
[186] *God among the Germans*, Douglass, p. 229.
[187] *God among the Germans*, Douglass, p. 223.

accepted it as inescapable, but with reservation or resentment."[188]

And later he writes: "It might also be said that the National Socialist leaders have found and will find that the Christian Church is an embarrassment. It cannot be fashioned as readily as are cultural institutions. They will find men whose convictions in their sphere are as unyielding as those of Hitler himself in the political realm. They have to be reckoned with."[189]

Confessional Christians (non-Nazi Protestants) opposed the Nazis very early indeed. By October 1934, the Confessional Synod began publicly comparing the Nazi religious leadership to Satan.[190] By the end of that year, as Lichtenberger writes: "The increase in the opposition movement was very great. At the end of 1934 it was estimated that out of 16,000 pastor there were scarcely 3,000 who had ranged themselves freely behind the banner of Bishop Muller [the Nazi bishop] while 13,000 or more were won to the ranks of the Confessional front or else observed an attitude of prudent expectancy."[191]

Power, in his book on *Religion in the Reich*, relates: "At Whitsundie, 1936, the Confessional Leaders sent Hitler himself a secret memorandum which asked, in effect: 'Do you, or do you not, want to de-Christianize the Church?' The memorandum made it plain that promise had not been kept. Was this with the connivance of the Party, or it spite of it? Why the Church was never allowed to answer publicly the accusations made against it? How far did the National-Socialist Weltanschauung impinge upon the Christianity of the Gospels? Justice, Concentration Camps, the creed of Blood and Soil, the activities of the Gestapo –

---

[188] *The New Church and the New Germany,* MacFarland, p. 1.
[189] *The New Church and the New Germany,* MacFarland, p. 167.
[190] *God among the Germans,* Douglass, p. 256.
[191] *The Third Reich,* Lichtenberger, p. 202.

all the vexed questions of the past years were raised and clearly put. In this document the Evangelical Church gave the Fuhrer a clear-cut opportunity to define once and for all, if he could, his attitude toward organized Christianity. There was no answer."[192] The rebellious Protestants of Germany took the great risk of asking straight questions for Hitler, and he simply ignored them.

Herman wrote about the resistance that Christians gave to Hitler: "Until the outbreak of the war, and even afterwards, the 'church story' was one of the biggest features of the news from Germany. All in all, it constituted the only significant and persistent resistance to Adolph Hitler during a dozen incredible years of mass hysteria, ruthless tyranny and insatiate aggression."[193]

This was the greatest domestic failure of the Nazis: "The German Fuhrer's colossal failures outweigh in every instance his colossal coups. His biggest failure inside the Reich was the failure to win the church. His most numerous, most vigorous and most persistent opponents from the first were men and women whose life and work were guided by the Gospel."[194]

Distinguished Jewish professors of college textbooks, like Salwyn Shapiro in his 1940 book, *Modern and Contemporary European History,* wrote: "The new Bishop believed in the principles of 'German Christianity' and proceeded to Nazify the church by revising the Bible to harmonize with Germanism and by insisting on the 'Aryan paragraph,' a regulation which demanded the elimination from the ministry of anyone of Jewish origin. Many Lutheran ministers refused to accept these changes on the ground that they were contrary to the principles of Christianity. A struggle followed between the government and the

---

[192] *Religion in the Reich,* Power, p. 139.
[193] *The Rebirth of the German Church,* Herman, p. xv.
[194] *The Rebirth of the German Church,* Herman, p. 28.

ministers, as a result of which many were ousted from their positions and persecuted. The problem of coordinating the Catholic Church was far more difficult because the Nazis had come to terms with the pope. A concordat was signed between Germany and the Vatican, according to which the Church was granted freedom in religious matters. However, conflict arose between the Nazis and the Catholics because the former violated the concordat. Catholic priests were attacked by Storm Troops, Catholic newspapers were suppressed, and Catholic schools were closed. In their ruthless policy of coordination the Nazis encountered only one opposition, that of the Protestant and Catholic clergymen, who bravely upheld their principles despite persecution."[195]

Professor Lichtenberger in his 1939 book, The Third Reich, writes: "In March 1935, the Confessional Synod of the Evangelical Church held at Dahlem solemnly accused National Socialism 'of setting up the myth of race and people, of making idols out of blood and race, nation, honor and liberty, in the place of God, and of demanding, as a new religion, faith in the eternal Germany and of wishing to supplant by this new faith in the eternal realm of our Lord and Saviour Jesus Christ.'"[196]

Lichtenberger goes on to explain how the Confessional Church has done it that it could to oppose the Nazis: "The Confessional Protestants defend themselves as best they can against this seizure [of power over religion by the state.] They reject as unholy the 'corrections' which the Nazis have made in traditional Christianity. They insist that *Wotanized* Christianity is no longer Christianity and that German Christians in rallying without reservation to the racialist doctrine had banished themselves from the community of the faithful. Finally, they refuse obedience to ecclesiastical superiors who do not, in their eyes, represent

---

[195] *Modern and Contemporary European History*, Shapiro, p. 857.
[196] *The Third Reich*, Lichtenberger, p. 201.

the community of the faithful but who were imposed from without the church by political authorities."[197]

This extended to the only sorts of opposition that the Christians in Germany could give: "The German Army for the first time in its history has marched into war without the blessing of the German Church. Of course, the benediction of all the pastors and priests goes along with the boys who leave for the front and sincere prayers are prayers for the security from harm and a safe return to their homes; both, in spite of formal petition for God's leadership of the Leader, what most Christian hearts are really asking God for is not a Nazi triumph but the miracle of a decent peace from enemies both within and without."[198]

Schuster notes in his 1935 book: "All that can be said is that nearly all the pastors as well as their loyal congregations did their duty. The spectacle was so reassuring that thoughtful persons everywhere took heart and felt that the life-blood of civilization still coursed in the veins of the German people. In New York, Dr. Alvin Johnson – who cannot well be accused of enthusiastic support for Christian Churches – told a distinguished gathering that the ideal of freedom could be saved for mankind only by those who believed strongly enough in a religion to be willing to die for it."[199] Power wrote: "In the Christianity of the German people, the National-Socialist has so far found the one enemy that it cannot vanquish."[200]

In 1938, Tabouis wrote in *Blackmail or War*: "Only a few brief references can here be made to the underground struggle against the Hitler regime. The extent of the Catholic opposition is being revealed more and more clearly in the sermons which are being preached from the pulpit, and

---

[197] *The Third Reich*, Lichtenberger
[198] *It's Your Souls We Want*, Herman, p. 251.
[199] *Like a Mighty Army*, Schuster, p. 120.
[200] *Religion in the Reich*, Power, p. 239.

also in the increasing number of people who take part in religious processions. During the summer of 1937 no less than 100,000 paraded at Annaberg in Silesia, while at Aix la Chapelle 50,000 resisted all the efforts of the police to disperse them. The Protestant opposition is equally staunch, in spite of wholesale arrests of clergy by the agents of the Gestapo. At the present time 86 pastors of the 'Confessional Church' are in German prisons, including one of the most popular of them, Pastor Niemoeller of Dahlem, who during the war was the commander of a submarine."[201]

In his 1938 book, *Germany Puts the Clock Back*, Mower describes how in 1933 freedom vanished, and how resistance to Nazis did not come from universities or science or art or literature or radio or newspapers but only from religiously serious people.[202]

Leo Stein, in his 1942 book, *I was in Hell with Niemoeller*, says that he is writing the book, in spite of the harm that might come to Niemoeller, because: "Whether it will result in greater hardships for him or not, I know that it is his wish that the world at large, and especially the people of America, should be enlightened as to the part he has played against the Nazi attempt to destroy Christianity throughout the world"[203] and later in the book he writes: "I could not but marvel at the spiritual strength of the man, who, as I have said, could have uttered one word of surrender and gained his freedom and probably a high place in the councils of the Nazi Party."[204] Max Dimont observed that Nazi propaganda had been anti-Christian since 1919, and that Jews sent to concentration camps were met there by

---

[201] Genevieve Tabouis, *Blackmail or War*, (Middlesex, England: Penguin, 1938), pp. 207-208.

[202] *Germany Puts Back The Clock*, pp. 242 – 243.

[203] *I was in Hell with Niemoeller*, Stein, p. 5.

[204] *I was in Hell with Niemoeller*, Stein, p. 63.

Christians of conscience who arrived before the Jews.[205]

As time passed, this resistance became more and more emphatic and the price that individual Christians were willing to pay grew increasingly heavier. Carl Friedrich Goerdeler was a devout Christian. Goerdeler strongly opposed Nazi anti-Semitism. In Liebzig, he tried to stop the boycott of Jewish businesses. When the Nazis in 1936 ordered the demolition of a monument to Felix Mendelssohn, the great Jewish composer (who converted to Christianity), Goerdeler tried to have it rebuilt. He traveled around the world, warning anyone who listened of the dangers of Nazism and was the person selected by the conspirators to overthrow Hitler in 1944 to be the new Chancellor of Germany. He was arrested, brutally tortured, and finally executed by the Nazis. To the end, as a Christian, he opposed them, even as he had from the beginning.

Claus von Stauffenberg, the German general who almost killed Hitler in late 1944, was a devout Catholic who because of his faith was deeply opposed to the persecution of the Jews and considered that Kristallnacht in 1938 brought great shame upon Germany. He was the man who tried to kill Hitler in 1944. Stauffenberg was, of course, arrested, tortured and executed. Stauffenberg's wife, Countess Nina, who was pregnant with the couple's fifth child, was sent to Ravensbruck concentration camp.

Ulrich von Hassell, although he joined the Nazi Party, wrote this in his diary about the same Night of Broken Glass: "I am writing under crushing emotions evoked by the vile persecution of the Jews after the murder of von Rath." Both these men were murdered by the Nazis after the assassination of Hitler failed. Germans and Christians did not sit quietly while Nazis murdered Jews.

Helmuth von Moltke, son and grandson of some of the

---

[205] Max Dimont, *Jews, God and History* (New York: Signet, 1962), pp. 377 – 378.

most famous German military leaders, easily could have become a bigwig in the Nazi Party, if he had chosen to do so. But von Moltke possessed strong Christian convictions and wrote in 1942: "Today, not a numerous, but an active part of the German people are beginning to realize, not that they have been led astray, but that what is happening is sin and they are personally responsible for each terrible deed that has been committed naturally – not in the earthly sense, but as Christians." In the same letter, von Moltke wrote that once he had thought that it was possible to be totally opposed to Nazism without believing in God, but now he declared that to be "wrong, completely wrong," and that only by believing in God could one be an opponent of the Nazis. Von Moltke was arrested and executed by the Nazis in January 1945. The trial of Count Moltke in 1944 during the roundup of opponents to Hitler after the assassination attempt are telling. During his trial, the judge Friesler told Moltke: "Only in one respect does National Socialism resemble Christianity: We demand the whole man."[206] After the trial, Moltke wrote: "I stood before Freisler...as a Christian and nothing else."[207] And in a letter to his wife, a few days before his execution, Moltke is emphatically clear about what motivated him to oppose Hitler: "So then all that is left is a single idea, how Christianity can prove a sheet anchor in time of chaos."[208]

Gustaf von Haften refused to join the so-called "German Christian" Church established by the Nazis and at great personal risk belonged to the real Christian Church, the Confessing Church. He supported the attempt to overthrow Hitler and, like all the other Christian martyrs, intervened whenever he could to protect Jews, to protest Nazi anti-Semitic policies and to help Jews escape. He was tried

---

[206] *German Opposition to Hitler*, Rothfels, p. 118.
[207] *German Opposition to Hitler*, Rothfels, p. 127.
[208] *German Opposition to Hitler*, Rothfels, p. 11.

and hanged by the Nazis in August 1944, where he described Hitler as the "executioner of evil in history."

Alfred Delp, who had entered the Society of Jesus, also tried to stop the persecution of Jews. He was arrested, tortured, placed in solitary confinement and finally executed in January, 1945. These few names are but the tip of the iceberg of devout Christians who chose to oppose Hitler because of their faith and who died a horrible, lonely death because of that faith.

Christians resisted the Nazis almost as soon as the Nazis came to power. In the end, Christians paid with their lives and the lives of their families, even though they were important Germans who would otherwise have been left alone, because the evil of Nazism was inconsistent with their faith. We have the words of these martyrs, which speak for themselves.

Chapter 7
Christians and Nazi Anti-Semitism

Any book that discussed the Nazi War on Christianity would be incomplete if it did not discuss the relationship between Christianity and Nazi anti-Semitism. The unhappy reality of Christian anti-Judaism is, historically, true. In *Sinisterism: Secular Religion of the Lie*, I chronicle the interrelationship between Jews and Christians from the earliest days of Christianity. Jewish anti-Christianism and Christian anti-Judaism both existed and in neither case was persecution the core of the problem. Jews viewed Christianity as heresy, which should be punished by death. Christians viewed Jews as "Christ-killers" and Judaism as incomplete Christianity. The history of Christian antipathy for Jews needs no elaboration here. Although never anti-Semitic (Christians believe that God, His Mother and all the disciples were Semitic Jews), it has been anti-Judaic and even, at different times in history, anti-Jewish. The history of Jewish antipathy for Christians has been just as real and, like just as Christians have on occasion massacred Jews, Jews have also massacred Christians – sometimes, as in Yemen in October, 523 [209]or the Holy Land in July,

---

[209]   Kevin Alan Brook, *The Jews of Khazaria* (New Jersey: Aronson Inc., 1999), p. 268.

614[210] this genocide has resulted in the murder of thousands or even hundreds of thousands of Christians. The methods of murder have also been horrific.[211]

During the last two centuries both Jews and Christians have recognized that their two faiths have in common a unique and good set of values. This has not meant that pogroms in Russia stopped, but it has meant that nearly the entire Christian world absolutely condemned these crimes as un-Christian. This has not meant that all Jews stopped viewing Christianity as a form of heresy, but has meant that many Jewish thinkers have begun to write publicly what many had long thought: Christianity, like Judaism, was a blessing to the world.

This became pronounced just as the Nazi threat was growing. Jewish authors like John Cournos, who wrote: "There are two ideas in the world today: Communism and Fascism, which would make us free, and Judaeo-Christianity, which would set us free"[212] and Sholem Asch, who wrote: "The dignity of the human being, that sacred position bestowed on him by the Judaeo-Christian religion, can be restored only by acceptance and submission to its teachings."[213] In his 1934 book, *The Rise and Destiny of German Jews*, Jacob Marcus the clear distinction between Christian Socialists and true anti-Semites: "Christian Socialists, as we have seen, wanted to destroy Jewish influence by assimilating the Jews more intimately into the life of the land; the other parties, truly anti-Semitic, wanted to get rid of all German Jews."[214]

The notion that Christianity gave rise to Nazism is

---

[210] Michael Grant, *The Dawn of the Middle Ages* (Maidenhead, England: McGraw-Hill Books, 1981), p. 140.

[211] Ibn Warraq, *What the Koran Really Says* (New York: Prometheus Press, 2002), p. 283.

[212] *An Open Letter to Jews and Christians*, Cournos, p. 29.

[213] *One Destiny*, Asch, p. 88.

[214] *The Rise and Destiny of the German Jew*, Marcus, p. 32.

wrong as the notion that Judaism gave rise to that identical twin of Nazism, Bolshevism. It is quite true that many of the early Bolsheviks were Jewish and that many Communists around the world were Jewish. It is also true that these Jews were anti-Judaic Jews who had contempt for their faith. As early as 1921, soon after the Bolsheviks came to power, authors were commenting upon this critical fact. Spargo, in his book, *The Jew and American Ideal*, observes that: "Trotsky has many times declared that he is not Jew, but a 'general proletarian,' and Bela Kun, in a formal statement, declared himself opposed to all religions and cultures, the Jewish included...Not only is Bolshevism fundamentally opposed to the Jewish religion; it is equally antagonistic to the principle of nationality itself." [215] He goes on to note that many of the Bolsheviks who were supposed to be Jewish were not and that many of the people who were Jewish and were listed as Bolsheviks were actually Jewish opponents of Bolshevism.[216]

The horror of the Holocaust, a crime perhaps unequalled in human history, has created rage among its victims which cannot be satisfied merely by the utter destruction of those who actually caused the Holocaust. None of us who have not lived through that nightmare should judge too quickly the sincerity of those actual victims of Nazi mass sadism. But truth, like vengeance, must also have a champion. Not only did Christians not cause the Holocaust, but Christians opposed the Nazi anti-Semitism which preceded the Holocaust.

Haters of Christianity and supporters of Nazis embraced the odious racial theories which led all Jews, whether they embraced Judaism or whether they embraced Christianity, to the death camps. The very issue of race, of

---

[215] Joe Spargo, *The Jew and American Ideal*, (New York: Harper and Brothers, 1921) p. 77.
[216] *The Jew and American Ideal*, Spargo, pp. 61-66.

anti-Semitism, rather than anti-Judaism, turned out to be the first direct conflict between Christians and Nazis regarding Jews. The religion of Jews was not important to the Nazis. The Jewish race was the enemy. One of the first measures the Nazis sought was to keep Jews who converted to Christianity out of the Christian Church. Theologically, this was completely at odds with Christian faith. It was precisely in keeping with the spirit of Nazism and paganism. So, Erich Ludendorff, the earliest and most important political figure in Germany to support the Nazis and also one of the most vicious opponents of Christianity, said: "The Jews are not our enemies because of their race, but because one of their subtlest rabbis, that man called Saint Paul, distilled the poison of the Christ myth out of the life of the story of Jesus of Nazareth. The Jews are enemies of the Nordic race because they produced Christianity, which has been the poison that has destroyed the vitality of the Aryan people."[217] Jews were hated most for bringing into the world Christianity. The "rabbi," Paul had destroyed the vitality of the Aryan people. This was not what Christians have ever thought, and this was manifested quickly in Christian opposition in Germany to any linking of religion and race.

But Christian opposition went beyond just opposing the inclusion of Christian Jews into the category of Jews. Schuster notes in his 1935 book that: "After Hitler had been lifted into the saddle, some eminent conservatives tried hard to call off the crusade against Jews"[218] and he goes on to observe that hatred of Jews was not endemic in Germany: "There was no dearth of goodwill toward Jews. It was for several reasons more prevalent among Catholics than Lutherans. The Center Party had good Jewish friends and appreciated them; various Catholic foundations were

---

217 *Days of Our Lives*, van Paassan, pp. 168 – 169.
218 *Like a Mighty Army,* Schuster, p. 76

befriended by Jews and did not forget to be grateful. A considerable number of intelligent Jews found the road to Rome, and some of them became relatively prominent. Among them were numbered writers, editors, teachers, priests and civil servants who were eminent in the days of the Republic. All things considered, the tone of the Catholic press was friendly to the Jews. Protestants were quite as courteous and interested."[219]

Christian Counter-Attack also notes that: "As early as 1933 Cardinal Faulhaber devoted a series of Advent sermons to condemning Nazi racialism, the new paganism and the persecution of Jews"[220] and "...when all others were fearful of helping the Jews because of Nazi threats, the Cardinal went to their aid at once, provided a lorry to remove religious objects from the Chief Rabbi of Bavaria's synagogue and stored them in his palace. The Nazis raised the cry 'Away with Faulhaber the friend of Jews,' and a mob raised his palace, but he was not intimidated."[221] Female German pastor Frau Staritz admonished Christians that those Jews who wore the Star of David must be shown special Christian charity under the Nazis.[222]

When the one day boycott of Jewish business took place in 1933, MacFarland recites what happened: "Pastors and local groups of pastors conferred and sought to exercise restraint. Individual leaders spoke out openly. There is good evidence that the limiting of the official boycott to one day was the result of church intervention. Officials of the World Alliance for Friendship through the Churches registered a declaration against the boycott. Dr. Hermann Kapler, at that time President of the German Church Federation, went at once to state officials with his protest

---

[219] *Like a Mighty Army,* Schuster, p. 88.
[220] *Christian Counter-Attack*, Martin et al., p. 24
[221] *Christian Counter-Attack*, Martin et al., p. 24
[222] *Christian Counter-Attack*, Martin et al., p. 41.

against violence – a step that anyone who knew him would take for granted. To what extent such protests were registered or given consideration, it is difficult to say."[223]

In July of the same year, the pastors of Berlin made it clear that they would not exclude Jews from the church, with the following appeal: "The exclusion of the Jewish Christians from our communion of worship would mean: The excluding Church is exercising a racial law as a prerequisite of Christian communion. But in doing so, it loses Christ himself, who is the goal of even this human, purely temporal law. The Christian Church cannot deny to any Christian brother the Christian communion which he seeks."[224]

In 1934, the World Baptist Congress "deplored and condemned as a violation of the law of God, the Heavenly Father, all racial animosity and every form of oppression or unfair discrimination against the Jews…"[225] This body of evangelicals, so often associated with narrow minded thinking by outsiders, without equivocation opposed Nazi anti-Semitism. Catholics felt the same. Freely, a Catholic priest, wrote in 1940 "With vicious worlds and more vicious deeds, Nazism boasts of its guilt in seeking to liquidate the Jewish people. Not only is it un-Christian to be anti-Semitic, but 'racism' (or intolerance of any alien races) is definitely against the teachings of Christ."[226] Soon after the Concordant between the Nazi regime and the Catholic Church, Essex and Dark observed: "The Church, too, courageously denounced the brutal and organized anti-Semitism."[227] *Christian Counter-Attack* notes: "Anti-

---

[223] *The New Church and the New Germany*, MacFarland, p. 76.
[224] *The New Church and the New Germany*, MacFarland, pp. 69-70.
[225] Michael Burleigh, *Sacred Causes*, (New York: HarperCollins, 2007), p. 208.
[226] *Nazism versus Religion*, Freely, p. 4.
[227] *The War Against God*, Dark, p. 201.

Semitism denies the Christian view of man."[228]

Christian Counter-Attack specifically notes the grounds for Christian opposition to anti-Semitism: "It was the assault of the Nazis upon spiritual values that drove the churches to resistance. The point at which conflict was joined varied from country to country: the flouting of elementary principles of justice, interference with the home or with the education of children, the euthanasia program, the anti-Semitic decrees."[229]

Heinberg wrote in his 1937 book on major European governments that the Pastor's Emergency League, an organization of some 3,000 pastors under the leadership of Pastor Martin Niemoeller, furnished strong opposition at the outset to the German Christian Church (a Nazi invention) and that the League membership doubled in November 1933 when the Nazis tried to keep Jewish members of the Christian churches segregated from non-Jewish Christians.[230] The reaction of Christians, when the Nazis tried to exclude "Jewish Christians" from Christianity was to join in increasing numbers the increasingly dangerous anti-Nazi Emergency League.

MacFarland told what happened, early in the reign of Hitler, about the Christian clergies attempt to oppose the racial element in Nazism: "A petition was conveyed to the National Synod on behalf of two thousand pastors which was also not considered. [by the Nazis] A group of outstanding theologians on September 23, 1933 issued the following judgment...1. According to the New Testament the Christian Church is a church of Jews and Gentiles visibly united in one communion. 2. According to the New Testament only faith and baptism are decisive for incorporation with the Church; Jews and Gentiles may equally be brought

---

[228] *Christian Counter-Attack*, Martin et al., p. 15.
[229] *Christian Counter-Attack*, Martin et al., p. 14.
[230] *Comparative Major European Governments*, Heinberg, p. 485.

to faith and baptism."[231] MacFarland also wrote that: "The year 1933 was characterized, as has been indicated, by strong declarations [by the Confessing Church] against the dangers of national self-deification and also by a categorical refusal to subscribe to the 'Aryan paragraph' with which Jewish persecution began."[232] Again, writers at the time (not later) were specifically identifying the Christian response to Nazi racialism and noting the unacceptability to Christians of Nazi anti-Semitism. At no point, really, did Christians ever endorse the racial hatred of the Nazis. At least as significantly, non-Christian Germans, who did embrace racism, were not at all perturbed by anti-Semitism. Christians, alone, were.

Power noted in this book that: "The Aryan paragraph in this new proposal, and the implications of a new creed in which racialism superseded Christian internationalism, drew an immediate and sturdy reaction from Protestantism. Dr. Otto Dibelius of Brandenburg (who was later to suffer for his temerity) retorted that the Gospel must be put before political ideology."[233] This position was not taken without personal risk.

The Catholic Church in Germany also addressed the Aryan question during the first year of Nazi power, and the Catholic response during the very first year of Nazi power was just as emphatic and clear: "We believe that national unity is to be realized, not exclusively by identity of blood, but also by identity of outlook and that the assertion of the single principle of race and blood, amongst the member of the same state, leads to injustices which outrage the Christian conscience."[234]

The stand of all Christians against the racial policies of

---

[231] *The New Church and the New Germany*, MacFarland, p. 74.
[232] *The Rebirth of the German Church*, Herman, p. 60.
[233] *Religion in the Reich*, Power, p. 109.
[234] *The New Church and the New Germany*, MacFarland, p. 85.

the Nazis were addressed early and clearly. It never changed. But that leaves open the question of how Christians reacted to Jews who embrace Judaism, which is a different question. Those Jews who embraced Christianity were in a particularly dangerous position: Jewish relief agencies, who would help unconverted Jews, offered no help at all to Jews who converted to Christianity. The Christian response to those Jews – Jews in Nazi eyes, but Christians in Christian eyes – meant that if real Christians in Germany did not help them, no one would. But were Christians, persecuted themselves, silent when Germans persecuted non-Christian Jews? No – and that is a qualified answer. The quiet sympathy for Jews was such that stories swirled around the Christian community: "An anecdote current at the time reveals something of the prevalent spirit. Once, so went the story, an anti-Semitic pastor had prefaced his sermon with the remark: 'If there be a Jew in this House of God, let him get up and leave.' No one got up; not one word was spoken. But the crucifix above the pulpit detached itself from the wall, and slowly disappeared. For the Saviour was a Jew."[235]

Very early in the Nazi reign of terror, the World Alliance for International Friendship through the Churches, at its meeting in Sofia stated: "In a feeling of brotherhood and responsibility with all the Churches of the world, while recognizing the right of every nation to safeguard the integrity of its own national life, we are nevertheless deeply concerned by the treatment inflicted upon people of Jewish origin and connection in Germany. We especially deplore the fact that the State measures against the Jews in Germany have had such an effect on public opinion in some circles that the Jewish race is considered to be an inferior race."[236]

---

[235] *Like a Mighty Army,* Schuster, p. 109.
[236] *The New Church and the New Germany*, MacFarland, p. 172.

In his 1943 book, *It's Your Souls We Want,* Stewart Herman describes the fundamental incompatibility between Nazi polices and Christianity. As this book indicated, anti-Semitism was not only one of the irreconcilable differences between Nazis and serious Christians, but the what would be called the Holocaust was too: "Incomplete as this itemization of anti-Christian measure may be, it cannot be concluded without mentioning certain Nazi policies which, while not aimed directly at the church, have struck at the accepted social standards of Christendom and are irreconcilable with the Christian ethic. Of these policies three will automatically occur to the mind of the reader: the (official) adoption of euthanasia or mercy-killing, the glorification of the unmarried mother, and the cold-blooded extermination of the Jews." [237] That recitation is not qualified by the religion which those Jews practiced. It deals with the Holocaust of Judaic and non-Judaic Jews.

What caused the churches to be in conflict with Nazi Germany? *Christian Counter-Attack,* a 1943 book, explains: "It was the assault of the Nazis upon spiritual values that drove the Churches to resistance. The point at which conflict was joined varied from country to country: the flouting of elementary principles of justice, interference with the home or with the education of children, the euthanasia killings, the anti-Semitic degrees."[238] Again, the reference to Christian opposition to anti-Semitic degrees is not limited to "Jewish Christians," but to all Jews, who would be collectively the victim of Hitler's odious racial policies.

The attacks on Nazi racialism continued even while the Christian Church itself was under increasing attack, with its clergy in concentration camps and its possessions seized by the Nazis. At Whisundie in 1936, in a memorandum addressed from the leaders of the Confessing Church to Hit-

---

[237] *It's Your Souls We Want*, Herman, p. 223.
[238] *Christian Counter-Attack*, Martin et al., p. 14.

ler, these Christians stated: "When blood, race, nationality and honor are regarded as eternal values, the first commandment obliges the Christian to refuse this valuation. When the Aryan is glorified, the World of God teaches that all men are sinful. If the Christian is forced by the Antisemitism (sic) of the Nazi Weltanschauung to hate Jews, he is, on the contrary, bidden by Christian commandment to love his neighbor."[239] It is hard to see a more direct attack on Nazi anti-Semitism: It is mentioned by name.

Former Nazi leader of Danzig, who left the movement, Herman Rauschning wrote "From an ethical standpoint there is no Jewish problem. No believing Christian and no humane-minded person can be an anti-Semite. Rosenberg and Ludendorff are right, if in nothing else, in their claim that the New Testament is inseparably connected with the Old, and we Christians with our Jewish heritage."[240] On the first page of the Introduction of his book, Rauschning warns that this "Third Reich" was a "holocaust."[241] Again, Rausching, without qualification, speaks of the problem with anti-Semitism. He also, in horrible prescience, uses the word "Holocaust" to describe the Third Reich.

Nazi persecution of Jews racketed up in stages. One of the most awful, inhumane jumps was in 1938. Support for persecuted Jews continued through the terrible year of Kristallnacht: "1938 was notable chiefly at the moment of the Czech crisis, and for another clear protest [by the Confessing Church] against the Jewish pogrom of that year."[242] During 1938, when Jews were persecuted most viciously: "Definite groups, such as Quakers and Protestants as well as Catholic societies, were engaged in very extensive relief efforts."[243] Herman wrote the following about Kristall-

---

239 *German Opposition to Hitler*, Rothfels, pp. 41-42.
240 *The Revolution of Nihilism*, Rauschning, p. 92.
241 *The Revolution of Nihilism*, Rauschning, p. xi.
242 *The Rebirth of the German Church*, Herman, p. 61
243 *German Opposition to Hitler*, Rothfels, p. 32.

nacht: "It cropped up again and again at every new and more serious anti-Semitic measure until now the Jews were to be totally excluded from the German community. Nevertheless the Confessional Brethren was adamant in its insistence upon protecting these brethren and I can personally testify that in Berlin, where I personally knew what was going on, the pastors acquitted themselves heroically."[244]

Hambloch in 1939 wrote that it was not mere chance that an anti-Christian movement in Nazi Germany should have happened alongside anti-Jewish persecution, noting that no contortion of Christianity could allow the persecution of Jews that the Nazis were inflicting, and that the Nazis were not even trying to reconcile their actions with Christianity.[245] Ronald Kain, in his 1939 book, *Europe: Versailles to Warsaw*, wrote that Nazi treatment of the Jews offended serious Christians.[246]

In the winter of 1940: "When the evicted Jews were first transported from Vienna in trainloads, it was reported that a 'Jewless' Vienna would be Austria's birthday gift to Hitler two months later. Shortly thereafter a number of Christian pastors were arrested because they showed 'too much interest' in the events in Vienna."[247]

As late as October 1941, when it was extremely dangerous for anyone to oppose the Nazis, much less to speak up for the Jews, Father Bernard Lichtenberg, Dean of the Cathedral of St. Hedwig in Berlin, offered up public prayers in church for the safety of the Jewish people. He made this announcement from the pulpit: "An inflammatory pamphlet anonymously attacking the Jews is being disseminated among the houses of Berlin. It declares that any German who, because of allegedly false sentimentality,

---

[244] *It's Your Souls We Want*, Herman, p. 178.
[245] *Germany Rampant*, Hambloch, p. 82.
[246] Ronald Kain, *Europe: Versailles to Warsaw*, (New York: H.W. Wilson Company, 1940), p. 23 – 26.
[247] *It's Your Souls We Want*, Herman, p. 231.

aids the Jews in any way, is guilty of betraying the people. Do not allow yourself to be misled by this un-Christian attitude, but act according to the strict commandment of Jesus Christ – Thou shalt love thy neighbor as thyself." Father Lichtenberg was arrested on October 23, 1941 for the crimes of having prayed for the Jews and having offered prayers for Jews. When Monsignor Litchenberg was arrested, he offered to be transferred to the Lodz ghetto.248 Although Lichtenberg, beloved by his flock, was "only" sentenced to two years in prison, on October 23, 1943 he died as he was being transported in "protective custody" in a cattle car on the way to Dachau.

When Stewart Herman left Germany after war broke out between Germany and America, he relates: "One of the last visitors I had before leaving Berlin a year ago was a German pastor who had joined in the Confessional struggle with gusto and carried a tremendous burden of work and responsibility for many years. Yet, when he heard of the recent wholesale massacre of Jews in Poland and in Russia, he said 'I can't stand it any longer. No matter how the war ends or when it ends, I am going to leave for America. My wife and I talked it over the other night. I'm not young any more but I can never be happy here in my own country.'"248

Father Otto Mueller helped Jews escape the Holocaust and, as a result, he was arrested and tortured to death at Berlin-Tegel Prison in 1944. An estimated 5,000 Catholic priests and monks were arrested by the Nazis for the opposition to Nazism and were sent to concentration camps during the Second World War; more than 2,000 of those Catholics died in the camps.249

Both Sigmund Freud and Albert Einstein, famous Jews who had previously had nothing but contempt for Christianity, publically applauded the Church for standing up to

---

248 *It's Your Souls We Want*, Herman, p. 295.
249 *Germans Against Hitler*, Prittie, pp. 369 – 371.

the Nazi for its defense of the Jews and noting that no one else in Germany or Occupied Europe was standing up to the Nazis.[250]

Christians, who themselves were facing a holocaust and who were placed themselves in smaller and more hopeless ghettos of Nazi society, were also the only people in Germany who were opposing the Nazi mistreatment and murder of Jews. Did Christians fail to save Jews? Christians failed to keep their own pastors out of concentration camps. Nazis hated Christians and would not listen to them.

At a time when Gandhi was urging the Jews of Europe to commit collective suicide, at a time when Moslems were applauding the extermination of the Jews, at a time when the Bolsheviks, even after the Nazis began to war against them, ignored the Holocaust, Christians publicly denounced the evil of anti-Semitism and condemned the Nazi policies toward Jews. The Holocaust and Nazi anti-Semitism was not the consequence of too much Christianity, but of too little Christianity.

---

[250] *Sacred Causes*, Burleigh, p. 212.

Chapter 8
Nazi Ideology and Judeo-Christianity

What we called the ideological spectrum is simply the invention of those who hate Judeo-Christianity and all that this moral and philosophical tradition represents. There is no "Right" in politics which, if pursued too far, leads to Nazism. The Nazis, the Bolsheviks, the Fascists and all those other isms which finds Jews, Christians, Judaism and Christianity indigestible all believe in the same godless, power-mad, systems of violence and dishonesty.

I have written an entire book, *Sinisterism: Secular Religion of the Lie*, which details exactly how historically the Nazis have been Bolsheviks who have been Fascists. This was noted by writers during the 1930s, when discussing Nazism. The odious German Christian movement and the German Faith movement, those anti-Christian and anti-Semitic varieties of Nazi "religion" are enemies of Judeo-Christianity which I simply call "Sinisterist," because that allows us to have a word that includes all the totalitarians, wherever they may have been placed on some mythical ideological spectrum.

Those today who hate Christians, Jews, America and Israel worship the same pagan pantheon. They are all sibling Sinisterists. It is impossible to build the Gulag on Torah. It is impossible to build Treblinka on the Cross. The Judeo-

Christian tradition is the only protection we have in life against these horrors. But those who hate Christians and Jews do not wish Christians to be seen as separate from Nazis (just as they do not wish Jews to be seen as separate from Bolsheviks), and so the "Far Right" has come to be synonymous with devout Christians.

If this reasoning was wrong, then you would expect to find Christians and Nazis mortal enemies. This is, of course, exactly what happened historically. Christians, alone, proved unconquerable by the Nazis. It can be said that Christians did not succeed in stopping Hitler, but it cannot be said that they did not try, often at great loss and nearly always as true martyrs (people who could have chosen to live, but who chose to die for the sake of goodness.)

Film, television and other elements of media and culture completely ignore this. How often, in films involving the Nazis, do we see Christian clergy rounded up by the Gestapo? Or how many times have we seen Hollywood showing Christian masses protesting against the Nazis, after the Nazis were in power? How many times have movies shown Nazi leaders mocking Christianity? The Nazi War on Christianity (and the Christian response to Nazis) is a politically inconvenient fact, (just as presumed Christian collaboration with Nazis is a very politically convenient myth.)

Look today at how any efforts to maintain symbols of Christianity in schools is crushed. Look at how school books are purged of religious portions. Look at how celebrities take potshots at Christianity, growing increasingly outrageous as they see that nothing happens for their slanders against Christianity. Compare what happened in Nazi Germany with what is happening now. What was happening in Weimar Germany and then in Nazi Germany is happening today in America.

This book does not pretend to cover all the different interactions and opinions of hundred of millions of people during the decades it covers. Rather, I have pointed to the uniform opinion of those authors who wrote about the Nazis and Christianity at the time when the Nazis were in power.

Christianity, Judaism and Judeo-Christianity (a term coined by Jewish writers in the 1930s) were viewed as the mortal enemies of Nazism (just as these were viewed as the mortal enemies of Bolshevism.) The Judeo-Christian moral and theological tradition was as incompatible with Nazism as it was with Bolshevism – both of which were simply manifestations of human evil.

Just as the Bolsheviks, so often accused of being a "Jewish conspiracy," gleefully closed down synagogues, suppressed the teaching of Hebrew and persecuted Jews, so the Nazis, so often accused of being sort off-beat variety of "Christians," gleefully denounced Christianity, sent pastors and priests to concentration camps, and persecuted true Christians.

In a world dominated by simmering and often boiling hatred for Judeo- Christianity, it is increasingly important for all the elements of Judeo-Christianity to unite. And these elements of Judeo-Christianity must unite under the common banner of truth. That is the simple purpose of this book.

Bibliography

Bayne, Stephan, *Understanding Jewish History,* (New York: Kvat Publishing, 1997)

Black, William Harman, *If I Were a Jew,* (New York: Real Book, 1938)

Brook, Kevin Alan, *The Jews of Khazaria,* (New Jersey: Aronson Inc., 1999)

Burleigh, Michael, *The Third Reich: A New History,* (New York: Hill and Wang, 2001)

Carmer, Carl, *The War Against God,* (New York: Henry Holt, 1943)

Collier, Price, *Germany and the Germans,* (New York: Charles Scribner's Sons, 1913)

Cournos, John, *An Open Letter to Jews and Christians,* (New York: Oxford University Press, 1938)

Dark, Sidney and Essex, R.S., *The War Against God,* (New York: Abington House, 1938)

Dimont, Max, *Jews, God and History,* (New York: Signet, 1962)

Douglass, Paul, *God among the Germans,* (Philadelphia: University of Pennsylvania Press, 1935)

Duncan-Jones, A.S., The Struggle for Religious Freedom in Germany, (London: Victor Gollancz, 1938)

Foder, M.W., *The Revolution is On!* (Boston: Houghton Mifflin, 1940)

Freely, Raymond , *Nazism versus Religion,* (New York: The Paulist Press, 1940)

Grant, Michael, *The Dawn of the Middle Ages,* (Maidenhead, England: McGraw-Hill Books, 1981)

Hamloch, Ernst, *Germany Rampant,* (New York: Carrick & Evans, 1939)

Harsch, Joseph, *Patterns of Conquest,* (Garden City, NY: Doubleday, Doran and Co., 1941)

Hoover, Calvin, *Germany Enters the Third Reich,* (New York: Macmillan, 1934)

Kain, Ronald, *Europe: Versailles to Warsaw,* (New York: H.W. Wilson Company, 1940)

Knox, Ronald, *Nazi and Narazene,* (London: MacMillan, 1940)

Lichtenberger, Henri, *The Third Reich,* (New York: The Greystone Press, 1937)

Loon, Henrik van, *Our Battle*, (New York: Simon & Schuster, 1938)

Lockhardt, R.H., *Guns or Butter?* (London: Putnam, 1938)

Lorimer, E.O., *What Hitler Wants*, (London: Penguin, 1939)

Lyon, Eugene, *The Red Decade*, (New Rochelle, NY: Arlington House, 1970), reprint of 1941 Bobbs-Merrill

Lowenstein,Karl, *Governments of Continental Europe*, (New York: Macmillan, 1941)

Lukács, John, *The Last European War*, (New Haven, CT: Yale University Press, 1976)

MacFarland, Charles, *The New Church and the New Germany*, (New York: MacMillan Company, 1934)

Macrakis Kristie, *Surviving the Swastika*, (Oxford, England: Oxford University Press, 1993)

Marcus, Jacob, *The Rise and Destiny of the German Jew*, (Cincinnati: Union of American Hebrew Congregation, 1934)

Martin, Hugh; Newton, Douglas; Waddams, H.M.; and Williams, R.R., *Christian Counter-Attack: Europe's Churches Against Nazism*, (London: Student Christian Movement Press, 1943)

Mossie, John, *The Myth of the Great War*, (New York: HarperCollins, 2001)

Mower, Edgar, *Germany Puts Back The Clock*, (New York:

William Morrow Company, 1939)

Myers, Gustavus, *The History of Bigotry in the United States*, (New York: Random House, 1943)

Overy, Richard, *The Dictators*, (New York: W.W. Norton, 2004)

Paassan, Pierre van, *Days of Our Lives*, (New York: Hillman-Curl, 1939)

Power, Michael, *Religion in the Reich*, (Oxford, England: Kemp Hall Press, 1939)

Rappoport, Angelo S., *The Gauntlet Against the Gospel,* (London: Skeffington & Son, 1937)

Rauschning, Herrman, *The Revolution of Nihilism*, (New York: Alliance Books, 1939)

Roberts, Stephan, *The House That Hitler Built*, (London: Methuen, 1939)

Rothfels, Hans, *German Opposition to Hitler*, (Hinsdale, IL: Regnery, 1948)

Rigg, Byran Mark, *Hitler's Jewish Soldiers,* (Lawrence, KS: University of Kansas Press, 2002)

Schapiro, Salwyn, *Modern and Contemporary European History*, (Cambridge, MA: The Riverside Press, 1940)

Schuster, George, *Like a Mighty Army,* (New York: Appleton-Century, 1935)

Spargo, Joe, *The Jew and American Ideal*, (New York:

Harper and Brothers, 1921)

Stewart, Herman, *It's Your Souls We Want*, (New York: Harper & Brothers, 1943)

Stewart, Herman, *The Rebirth of the German Church,* (New York: Harper Brothers, 1946)

Stein, Leo, *I was in Hell with Niemoeller,* (New York: Fleming Revell, 1942)

Tabouis, Genevieve, *Blackmail or War*, (Middlesex, England: Penguin, 1938)

Thompson, Dorothy, *Let the Record Speak*, (Boston: Houghton-Mifflin, 1939)

Valtain, Jan, *Out of the Night,* (Garden City, NY: Garden City Publishing Company, 1942)

Warraq, Ibn, *What the Koran Really Says,* (New York: Prometheus Press, 2002)

Weinrich, Max, *Hitler's Professors: The Part of Scholarship in Germany's Crimes Against the Jewish People*, (New York: Yiddish Scientific Institute, 1946)

Wolfe, Henry, *The German Octopus*, (New York: Doubleday, 1938)

Wythe, William and Parry, Albert, *Riddle of the Reich*, (New York: Prentice Hall, 1941)

CPSIA information can be obtained at www.ICGtesting.com
Printed in the USA
LVOW121726280912

300767LV00001B/206/P